D1328077

I ALL SAINTS' CHURCH, HASTINGS (OIL) BIRMINGHAM ART GALLERY

BRITISH PAINTERS SERIES

# DAVID COX

## TRENCHARD COX

*Director of the City Museum and Art Gallery, Birmingham*

WITH 54 ILLUSTRATIONS
INCLUDING 4 COLOUR PLATES

PHOENIX HOUSE LIMITED, LONDON
1947

PRINTED IN GREAT BRITAIN

Made 1947 in Great Britain
Printed at Prescot by C. Tinling & Co. Ltd. for
PHOENIX HOUSE LIMITED
38  WILLIAM  IV  STREET,  LONDON

*First published in Great Britain 1947*

# ACKNOWLEDGMENTS

In the preparation of this book I am in the debt of many people who have given me access to material relating to David Cox. Particularly I am grateful to the authorities of those museums and art galleries who have furnished me with information about, and have permitted me to reproduce, some of the paintings in their charge; and to the Secretary and the Librarian of the Royal Academy who placed at my disposal relevant material in their archives. Also, I express appreciation of help given by Sir Robert Witt, C.B.E., who allowed me to illustrate three drawings by Cox from his own collection as well as placing at my disposal the invaluable resources of his library of photographs. In Birmingham I gained much useful information from Mr W. E. Hardwick, M.B.E., who has made a special study of the history of Harborne ; and I acknowledge my indebtedness to Mr M. Brown, the owner of the water-colour reproduced as pl. 12. To my wife and to members of the staff of the Birmingham Art Gallery, who have helped in all the various stages of the formation of the book, I owe some very special thanks.

DECEMBER, 1946                                    TRENCHARD COX

42995

*Study of Courtyard at Haddon Hall*

# CONTENTS

# COLOUR PLATES

# MONOCHROME ILLUSTRATIONS

NOTE : The originals of the *Studies* illustrated in the text are in the Birmingham Art Gallery.

*Study of a cock*

# INTRODUCTION

# THE PAINTER'S INHERITANCE

THE BIOGRAPHY OF A CREATIVE ARTIST CANNOT BE NEATLY defined between the milestones of birth and death since many factors affecting his life form part of the inheritance which he derived from his parents or from the masters of his craft whom he most closely studied; and his position in the history of art must be also assessed by the influence he exerted on his contemporaries and successors. The characters of all human beings are formed by the interplay of impulses inherited from their forefathers but, in the case of an artist, this development is complicated by the clash of his urge for creation with the demands of external circumstance. The problem, often the tragedy, of an artist's life is the adjustment of these rival claims; the ruthless, lonely growth of genius which, in its highest potential, transcends time and place, cannot be reconciled with the transitory affections and responsibilities which fetter the common man. The compromise which every artist must work out for himself determines the whole trend of his life and work. In Turner is exemplified the genius whose private life seemed mysterious and shadowy even to his contemporaries, and who is now remembered as a timeless phenomenon of art rather than as a man, whereas in Cox the egotistical claims of the artist were too often subordinated to the kindly humanity which characterized him as a family man, friend and teacher. Turner was the master of his age, who could compel admiration for flights of lyricism which raised to the level of poetry such prosaic subjects as a railway engine or a municipal banquet. Cox, on the other hand, was the servant of his time; earning a hard living by teaching his craft to young ladies desirous of becoming 'accomplished', and producing pictures suitable for the drawing-rooms of the middle classes made suddenly wealthy by the Industrial Revolution. Only towards the end of his life was Cox free from economic pressure and able to paint for his own satisfaction, but painting was by that time so much a profession with him that only occasionally did his genius, as distinct from a high degree of craftsmanship, appear.

David Cox loved the countryside for its own sake and was content to subject himself to nature. His landscape painting is more often descriptive than interpretative; consequently, his vision of nature usually corresponds closely with that of the ordinary observer and his paintings are among those most easily enjoyed by the average man. If there is a single quality which may be said to characterize the work of Cox it is, perhaps, its essential 'Englishness', and this, though in one sense narrowing, denotes the presence of a national flavour without which few works of art are entirely successful. Cosmopolitanism is an overrated virtue, and exaggerated praise of it is mere inverted jingoism. A backward glance through the history of British painting is enough to show what was lost in those periods when the foreigner was encouraged only because he came from abroad.

During the seventeenth and through a great part of the eighteenth century there was little demand for English work. Lely and Kneller set a standard for aristocratic portraiture which was elegant and attractive but often lacked character, and the barbed wit of Hogarth was needed to expose the follies of a snobbery which would only allow opportunity to an English portrait painter if there were no foreigner at hand. Landscape painters were in a worse plight. Wilson's Welsh landscapes were a drug in the market; he could only find a sale for his pictures of foreign scenery; and Gainsborough, a passionate lover of the country, was obliged to concentrate on portraiture, whilst his unsold landscapes lay stacked at Schomberg House because patrons of art were not yet able to appreciate the great landscape painter who had come into their midst.

The main credit of directing the eyes of art lovers to the contemplation of the beautiful English landscape cannot, therefore, be given to the patrons (as late as 1761 Horace Walpole rather naïvely expressed surprise that a country so richly endowed with natural amenities should have produced so few landscape artists) but to the topographical draughtsmen who, throughout the eighteenth century, travelled far and wide in England, sketching and recording architectural antiquities and the country seats of the nobility. In the last quarter of the century and as the preachings of Rousseau created a fashion for the pastoral and romantic moods, the taste for topography reached its height with a constant succession of published works. Prints and books of landscapes were bought in increasing quantities, and in 1774 Messrs Wedgwood and Bentley completed a vast table service of their noted cream ware, commissioned by the Empress Catharine of Russia, on each piece of which was an English view, there being 1,282 views in all. The exhibition of this spectacular service in the firm's showrooms in Greek Street, Soho, before it was despatched to Russia, attracted great crowds and gave further impetus to the production of topographical art. Views of towns, ruins and 'gentlemen's seats' had become part of the regimen of elegant taste, and collections of prints were published to satisfy this social need. *The Copper Plate Magazine*, published monthly from 1777–8, and 1792–1802, contained, when complete, in addition to portraits and historical pictures, over forty 'select views in England and Wales'. In 1778 *The Virtuosi's Museum* was designed on similar lines and published by the same house, Messrs Kearsley of Serjeants' Inn. In competition, in 1779, W. Watts published *The Seats of the Nobility and Gentry*.

The heyday of the popularity of the topographical print was reached in the early years of the nineteenth century when a high degree of excellence in production and salesmanship was attained by a German resident in London, Rudolph Ackermann, coach-designer, publisher, dealer and drawing master. In 1808 he produced the first instalment of his *Microcosm of London*, with hand-coloured aquatints by Rowlandson & Pugin; this was followed in the succeeding year by the first issue of the *Repository of the Arts* which was to continue in three successive series of monthly numbers for the next nine years.

Thus was firmly established a fashion for large and luxurious volumes which started as *éditions-de-luxe* for the fastidious and declined into the plush-bound albums which adorned the best Victorian drawing-room tables and were mainly intended to provide edifying entertainment for the family at the fireside.

These topographers and publishers of engravings may indeed claim to have prepared the way for the British landscape school, and from their ranks emerged, and by them were employed, some of the painters of genius who made English water-colour painting a unique feature of European art.

One of the most accomplished of these adventurous spirits was Samuel Scott (1710–1772), best known for his marine pictures and London views in oils, but wisely admired by Horace Walpole for his 'washed drawings'. Scott might be called the father of the English school of water-colours, a title usually given to Paul Sandby (1725-1809), an inveterate sightseer and traveller in the British Isles, who exceeded the limits of a mere topographer (he contributed most of the drawings for the *Copper Plate Magazine*) by the range of his subject and the vigour and variety of his treatment. The first of the great masters of water-colour was born in the next generation, J. R. Cozens (1752-*c*.1799), who gave to his medium a spaciousness and beauty which inspired his successors. Constable described Cozens' art as 'all poetry' and ranked him as the greatest genius who had

*12*

touched landscape. Cozens provides a link with the wealthy patrons whose education in art was shaped by the Grand Tour. It was customary for such men to take a draughtsman with them on their journeys (they had, indeed, a distinguished precedent in Sir Walter Raleigh for, among the small band of pioneers whom he took to found the first English colony in North America in 1585, was John White, the earliest known English water-colour painter). John Smith about 1778 accompanied the Earl of Warwick to Italy (hence his sobriquet of 'Warwick' Smith); Thomas Hearne, from 1771 for over three years worked for the Governor of the Leeward Islands and William Pars went to Greece between 1763 and 1766 to make studies for the *Society of Dilettanti* which were engraved and published in Chandler and Revett's *Ionian Antiquities* in 1769; J. R. Cozens travelled in 1776 to Switzerland and Italy with Richard Payne Knight, and in 1782 went on a tour through Central Europe to Italy with William Beckford, the result of which was no 'minuting' (as Walpole described the topographer's function) nor a series of grandiose set-pieces, but compositions of the utmost nobility and subtlety.

Two artists who conferred the most exquisite grace upon the water-colour medium, Thomas Girtin (1775–1802) and J. M. W. Turner (1775–1851), began their careers as architectural draughtsmen. In their youth they sat together in the print publishing establishment of John Raphael Smith, and Girtin, in his mere twenty-seven years of life, always lived much as the average topographer of his time; but his tender romantic spirit and Turner's dazzling vision transformed the water-colour school. They, with John Sell Cotman (1782–1842), perhaps the most original designer of them all, raised the art to a peak of excellence which it has never reached again. By these outstanding artists the whole status of British water-colour painting was changed from that of a portfolio record or an *aide-mémoire* to a work of art which, regardless of size, could be matched as a mural decoration with the finest picture in oils. Paradoxically, the widened scope given

*13*

to the medium was partly a cause of its decline since, inasmuch as the popularity of water-colours increased, so were the few fastidious patrons replaced by an indiscriminate public who were not trained to appreciate essential differences in the two media. In order to give importance to his exhibition work Paul Sandby used the opaque method (water-colour and body colour) and reserved the transparent method (in which the surface of the paper contributes to the effect) for the work done for engravings. The growing success of public exhibitions strengthened the tendency to overwork water-colour and tempted artists to paint 'exhibition pictures'. The Royal Academy was largely to blame by insisting that water-colours should be framed like oils, although, in the early part of the nineteenth century, the organizers of the Academy exhibitions broke with precedent by allotting a separate room to water-colours. The foundation of the Society of Painters in Water-colour in 1804 gave official recognition and a sense of security to these painters, but it encouraged 'exhibition mania' in the public and tempted artists to give their work a 'finished' aspect which would challenge comparison with oils; indeed a dangerous example was set by Turner whose genius often enabled him to succeed where others failed.

A change in taste, which appears to modern eyes a decline, was affecting all the visual arts as the nineteenth century developed. The stately simplicity and aristocratic detachment of the preceding era were being gradually superseded by the emphasis on solid 'worth' and sentimental fussiness which found its apogee in the late Victorian age, when Chippendale chairs had been banished to the attics to make room for Chesterfields and sociables. Instead of a few oil paintings or colour-prints, water-colours, hung four deep and heavily mounted in gilt, were the obligatory ornaments for a properly furnished drawing-room. Cox, indeed, in spite of his intrinsic sincerity, could not escape from supplying the demands of fashion, nor is there any proof that he even wished to do so for, with his orderly, analytical mind and his inherited respect for craftsmanship,

*14*

he probably found it less irksome to conform to public taste than would a more strongly individual artist.

Both in time and place David Cox was born on the threshold of the Industrial era, of which his native city of Birmingham was a product. The grimy mediocrity of most of the surviving architectural relics of that epoch tends to make us disregard the sense of expectation with which men of imagination, scientists and artists alike, probably greeted a period of infinite mechanical and social possibilities. The immense wealth and power which machines placed at the disposal of man might have created another Renaissance with beautiful cities, enlightened artistic patronage and a well-ordered civic life, but the reality was one of crowded ugliness from which everyone longed to escape either in fact or in imagination. This escapism led to the demand for landscapes of a pleasant kind, preferably without any reminders of the pressing human problems which surrounded their purchasers. The pictorial potentialities of the industrial scene, which has attracted many painters of to-day, very rarely inspired the old masters of water-colour. *The Iron Forge between Dolgelly and Barmouth* was aquatinted by Paul Sandby and published in 1776; and one of John Sell Cotman's early masterpieces represented 'Bedlam Furnace' (now in the Hickman Bacon Collection, and painted about 1802). Although Cox felt more than his normal share of benevolence towards his fellow beings there is little interest in humanity shown in his work, and his figures are mostly types rather than character studies. The old woman who is seen from the back in so many of Cox's pictures, as she trudges along with her cloak billowing in the wind, is used purely as an element in the composition like any stump or stone.

One of the most endearing qualities in Cox's character was his unpretentiousness which, although compelling human sympathy, imposed limitations upon his art. He probably never aimed at doing more than giving pleasure, which is what he almost invariably succeeds in doing. Few people could feel that their experience of life

*15*

had been greatly widened or deeply enriched by Cox's pictures, but equally few could fail to derive from them some quiet satisfaction given by the artist's sympathetic understanding of nature. Cox never painted a commentary on life nor raised an intellectual problem, but he expressed his own belief in benign beauty, even in storm and wilderness, in contrast to the melodramatic terrors with which the eighteenth century romantics tended to invest the wilder aspects of nature. Both as an artist and as a person Cox was entirely free from cynicism and sophistication: a quiet, likeable man who took life as he found it and never questioned the ultimate justification of God's mysterious ways.

*Study of a man on horseback*

II BUCKINGHAM HOUSE FROM THE GREEN PARK (WATER-COLOUR) BIRMINGHAM ART GALLERY

# I

# BIRMINGHAM

## *1783-1804*

WHEN DAVID COX WAS BORN IN DERITEND, IN 1783, BIR-
mingham was little more than a market town retaining some of the
amenities still associated with that pleasant feature of English life.
Red brick buildings of the 'modern' Georgian type were replacing
the timbered houses which served as a reminder of the City's propin-
quity to the country; and in and near the Bull Ring (now the heart
of the business centre) were two covered market crosses used for the
sale of country produce. The affluence which was to accrue to
Birmingham with the rise in power of the manufacturer was not yet
a characteristic of the City which, in a census taken in 1781, could
boast of only thirty-six private carriages.

Deritend (originally the deer-gate end of Arden forest) had
become a poor suburb on the south-east side: a tiny community of
some five streets, one of which was Heath Mill lane, noted only as
being the scene of Cox's birth on the 29th April and as the site of
an ancient gabled inn, the Old Crown, which was mentioned in
Leland's Itinerary in 1531 and still exists. Joseph Cox, the artist's
father, was a blacksmith and whitesmith, and he foreshadowed the
contribution which Birmingham was to make to the armament of
future wars by forging bayonets, gun barrels and other weapons used
in the war against France.

David inherited from his father a respect for fine craftsmanship
which not only characterizes him as an artist but as a native of

B

Birmingham where technical skill is greatly prized. The unbroken popularity of the Pre-Raphaelite artists in Birmingham is a manifestation of the value set upon workmanship. The wider opportunities offered to David Cox as an artist did not eclipse his family pride, and in later life he liked to tell his friends how he would examine the bayonets of soldiers on patrol in the London parks in search for his father's trademark and of his pleasure when one day he discovered a horseshoe bearing his father's initials.

Joseph Cox was a worthy citizen, but with little education: his first wife, David's mother, came from a more prosperous home (her father was a miller) and she exerted a helpful influence upon her son who expressed gratitude to her for instilling into him principles which he never ceased to value. David's sister, Mary Ann Ward, married into a position superior to her own, her husband being an organist and teacher of music at Manchester. The family ties were never broken by David as his commitments increased: he paid an annuity to his father until his death in 1829 or 1830, and at intervals visited his sister in Lancashire who reciprocated by frequent visits to Cox at Harborne after the death of her husband.

The limited resources of the Cox family did not allow for any education for David other than the most elementary kind, and at the age of six or seven he went to a simple day school. At this period occurred an accident which must have seemed at the time little more than an irritation affecting domestic routine, but which may have led to the enrichment of British art. David tripped over a door-scraper one dark evening and broke his leg. During his convalescence a cousin, one Allport* gave the boy a box of colours with which he amused himself by painting paper kites brought to him by his school

---

*This Allport may have been a son of John Allport, a 'painter in general' of No. 54, Bull Street, Birmingham; or he may have been an artist of the same name, a pupil of John Glover, who, together with a son of Glover, opened in 1808 an academy of drawing for young ladies in Bull Street. A further possibility is that he was identical with Henry C. Allport who became a member of the Old Water-colour Society in 1818.

fellows. It is said that David had already shown some skill with his pencil; and now to pass the long hours in bed he copied some prints which he sold to friends for trifling sums. His gratified parents were thus made aware of their son's keenness for designing, and after a short period at the Birmingham free school and a testing time in his father's workshop where it was found that his health would not stand the strain, they decided to apprentice him to one of the toy-makers then flourishing in the City. As a preliminary David was sent for drawing to a night school kept by Joseph Barber where Newhall and Edmund Streets unite. Among his fellow pupils were Charles and Joseph Vincent Barber, sons of the artist, and Samuel Lines, noted for his topographical drawings of Birmingham. Barber was a stern disciplinarian, and insisted that his pupils should draw correctly; to achieve this they had to repeat the same subject many times, but this deadening process did not kill David's enthusiasm for his craft, and may have established the painstaking attitude which he always adopted towards his work.

The firm to which David was first apprenticed was started about 1775 by Mr John Taylor who manufactured buttons, buckles, snuff-boxes and bric-à-brac, which were painted and enamelled. The work done there may have been unpretentious, but the output must have been great, as one member of the staff is recorded as having earned three pounds ten shillings a week by painting the tops of snuff-boxes at the rate of one farthing each. If this were true it would imply some method of mass-production as the weekly total for one man would have been 3,360, a physical impossibility! During this period it seems that David began his expeditions into the country, which were to become so predominant a feature of his life, for among the papers of J. J. Jenkins, Secretary to the Old Water-colour Society, is a record of his having seen, carved on the wall of Guy's Cliff Mill, Warwickshire, the inscription 'David Cox, 1795'. One wonders whether when the boy of twelve committed this solecism he took a sketchbook with him?

At the age of fifteen David was accepted as apprentice to a locket and miniature painter in Birmingham, one Fieldler (or possibly Fielder), with whom he studied the art of painting lockets and decorating box lids with scenes taken from Dutch pictures. His precocity must have been considerable, as a locket, painted with the head of a young man, shows a facility most surprising in the work of a mere lad, and is executed with an accuracy which would have satisfied Barber. This miniature, formerly in the possession of David Cox junior, was lent to the Victoria and Albert Museum by the Rev H. G. Hills. As the costume of the sitter is of an earlier date the miniature is probably a copy of an unknown original. Again an accident—this time a tragedy—suddenly deflected Cox's career into a new course. After some eighteen months of apprenticeship, one day, on arriving

1 THE TERRACE AT HADDON HALL    (WATER-COLOUR)    BIRMINGHAM ART GALLERY

for work, he found the body of Fieldler who had hanged himself; and the shock of this nauseating discovery added to David's mental disquietude about the loss of his job. The beneficent cousin Allport provided the solution by obtaining for him the humble position of colour-grinder and general help in the scene-painters' loft at the Birmingham theatre. This must have seemed a thrilling adventure to any boy attracted by the glamour of the stage: furthermore, it enabled him to resume for a time his evening attendances at Mr Barber's school.

The lessee and manager of the theatre was Macready, father of the famous tragedian, William Charles Macready; and David worked for his chief scene-painter, James de Maria, a scenic artist of great repute, who had come from the Opera House in London, and had accompanied Turner on his wanderings in Devonshire. De Maria's panorama of Paris, painted from sketches made from one of the towers of Notre Dame, drew crowds to the Haymarket in 1802 when the critics declared it to resemble the painting of Richard Wilson. Cox also used to compare de Maria's settings with paintings by Wilson and Claude, which indicates how persistently the classical landscape tradition affected theatrical decoration.

David Cox was far too artless a personality to be deeply affected by the artifices of the stage, but there are traces of his early training in some of his later landscapes. For instance a water-colour 'The Terrace at Haddon Hall', p. 20, in the Birmingham Collection (No. 291/25) would make an admirable stage tableau. Throughout his life Cox retained an admiration for his master de Maria (whom he described as a 'very clever fellow indeed'), and some forty years later when in the Knole woods at Sevenoaks, he was reminded of his scenery and remarked to a friend how much he would like to see it again. At a chance encounter at the exhibition of the Water-colour Society in 1813, Cox expressed to de Maria how much he felt himself indebted to him in matters of art, whereupon the old artist assured him that he had now a great deal to learn from the boy who had once ground his colours.

*21*

Soon after arriving at the Birmingham theatre David made friends with the chief carpenter to whom he confided his love of drawing and painting: this reached the ears of de Maria who set him to work on some of the side scenes. David began on a 'flat' representing some country folk at a fair, one of whom was having his pocket picked; and his lively rendering of the scene induced de Maria to give him further work. David's first little success occurred when Macready put on a play of which the plot revolved around a portrait of the heroine, acted by a certain Miss Decamps. No one could be found to paint the picture and David, encouraged by his training as a miniature painter, offered very humbly to try his hand. His promptness and enterprise saved the play and impressed Macready, who made him one of his principal scene-painters, not only in the Birmingham theatre but in other provincial playhouses under his management. In this way, David, now a youth of eighteen or nineteen, would travel about with the players to such centres as Bristol, Sheffield, Manchester, Liverpool, or in smaller places where they sometimes gave performances in extemporized theatres, thereby calling upon the utmost ingenuity from their scene-painter. It is said, indeed, that David had occasionally to take a minor part in the play, and once in some country town he acted the rôle of pantaloon.

Macready's son was then a child, and David painted for him a sequence of scenes for a toy theatre which had been constructed for the boy by a stage carpenter. One of the scenes represented a flock of sheep being driven to market and the sheep were made to move by an ingenious device of rollers. Macready never forgot his pleasure in this fascinating toy and, about fifty years later, when a celebrated actor, he subscribed two guineas towards Cox's testimonial portrait as a mark of his grateful esteem.

Cox, although adroit as a scene-painter, was never temperamentally suited to the life of the theatre. His solid working-class upbringing did not fit him for bohemian ways, and he was revolted by the squalor and discomfort which touring companies had at that time to

*22*

endure. The petty dishonesties and jealousies among members of the troupe distressed him, and he found consolation in spending as much of his spare time as possible in the quiet company of the Barbers with whom he drew from life and sketched from nature. His association with Macready ended with a quarrel, the precise nature of which is unknown. Some say that Macready was under the impression that a certain piece of scenery was not by Cox and remarked to Cox, who had painted it, that it was far better than anything he (Cox) could produce; others recount the more generally accepted story that, in announcing a new play, the bills advertised 'entirely new and brilliant scenery by that unrivalled artist, Mr Daubeney of London', whereas in fact David Cox had executed the work attributed to the Londoner. Whatever the slight it resulted in a protest from the very modest David, who decided to terminate his engagement at the theatre as soon as he could be released. In this he was supported by his parents who were prejudiced against his theatrical connexions; and David is reputed to have shown a pressing letter from his mother to Mrs Macready who used her influence in liberating him from his contract with her husband. About this period Astley, the proprietor of a circus, was in Birmingham, and offered to employ David at Lambeth. With many misgivings and accompanied by his mother, who must have hoped against hope that her son, now just twenty-one, would not become further entangled in theatrical enterprise but achieve his desire to be a landscape painter, David set off, on a summer's day in 1804, by coach to London where he was to find, if not fortune, fame.

*Study of Whitehall*

# II
# LONDON
## *1804-1814*

HIS MOTHER'S FEARS THAT DAVID'S CAREER AND MORAL character would be jeopardized by theatrical life in London did not materialize. If his employment with Astley ever took place it was intermittent, and there are various explanations given as to why he did not take the chances offered to him by the circus proprietor. One is that Astley, completely ignorant of the principles of painting, asked Cox to paint a drum of which both ends could be seen at once: another story tells that, with his characteristic diffidence, he shrank from joining a company which already contained other artists. However, Cox seems not to have severed completely his connexion with the stage, as he was commissioned to paint scenes for the Surrey and Swansea theatres and, as late as 1808, he was paid by the manager of the Wolverhampton Theatre for painting 310 yards of scenery at the rate of 4s. a yard.

On arrival in London the Coxes found respectable lodgings near the Elephant and Castle where, in due course, David married his landlady's daughter, Mary Ragg.* Her family connexions were such as would have reassured Mrs Cox, who confided David to the kindly care of Mrs Ragg before returning to the Midlands. Charles Barber (who afterwards was twice President of the Liverpool Academy)

---

*In *Cox the Master* Mr F. Gordon Roe states that there is reason to believe that Mrs Cox's maiden name was Agg, not Ragg, which is commonly given by most of Cox's biographers.

followed David Cox to London. He and Richard Evans, later to paint duplicates of royal portraits for Sir Thomas Lawrence P.R.A., became firm friends with Cox and the three used to go out sketching together.

As soon as David had settled down in London he began to explore every opportunity of becoming a professional artist. He offered a number of sketches and drawings in sepia or Indian ink to a dealer named Simpson in Greek Street, Soho, who sold them principally to drawing-masters to be used as copy for their pupils. The remuneration to Cox was in inverse ratio to his enthusiasm; and he would in later life relate how he sold his early drawings at the price of two guineas a dozen. With some of his earnings Cox subscribed to the *Liber Studiorum* and thus established an admiration for Turner which he never relinquished. Also, as a standard for composition, Cox purchased a series of etchings after Gaspar Poussin, Salvator Rosa and Claude Gellée, published by Pond in 1741, 1744, and 1746; these he would faithfully work upon by copying them in water-colour: a practice commonly adopted by struggling artists, including Turner who, according to Dayes 'acquired his professional powers by borrowing where he could a drawing or picture to copy from, or by making a sketch from any one in the Exhibition early in the morning and finishing it at home'. *The most constructive opportunity for study was provided by Simpson who permitted Cox to copy a painting by Gaspar Poussin, in his possession, representing a flock of sheep in a landscape with ruins. Inspired by this Cox made a large drawing in water-colour of Kenilworth Castle, which was probably executed about 1806 or 1807 and must rank perhaps as Cox's earliest important work.† A preliminary study for the drawing is the 'Kenilworth Castle,' p. 27, (No. 323/07) in the Birmingham Collection. It is painted in pale, flat washes and suggests a lyrical mood often absent from the

---

* Finberg, A. J. *The life of J. M. W. Turner*, Oxford, 1939.  † Reproduced in *Solly*, pl. V.

2A KENILWORTH CASTLE (SKETCH IN WATER-COLOUR) BIRMINGHAM ART GALLERY

artist's mature development. Indeed, the little drawing reflects Cox's association with the theatre for the atmosphere is one of fantasy and the fresh air painting for which Cox became so noted has not yet come into being. A replica of Cox's first major drawing, signed by him and dated 1830, is in the Lady Lever Art Gallery, Port Sunlight (No. 342), p. 28. It indicates Cox's fidelity to past associations. He painted the castle many times and at various stages of his career, but it had a special attraction for him as being the subject which first gave him assurance as a painter; and it is characteristic of him—and rather touching—that some twenty years later he reproduced the composition which, in youth, he had executed partly as an exercise and partly as a tribute to a famous painter of the past.

27

28

In search of subjects for drawings Cox and his companions used to explore old London, and he was particularly attracted by the Thames and its surrounding buildings. A delicate water-colour at Birmingham 'Old Westminster', p. 30, (No. 347/07) bearing the date 1805, is a record of his youthful wanderings; in it the artist shows a breadth of treatment combined with a lightness of touch which the popular demand for the more fussy detailed landscape did not encourage him to retain. It is an exceedingly efficient, yet sensitive architectural study and, in the opinion of Mr Finberg, 'might almost pass for a Girtin'. The paint is laid on with a very thin wash but the solidity of the architecture is clearly indicated, and the Abbey is shown, rising above the old houses in its precincts, in truly monumental grandeur. As well as to Simpson, Cox would offer his drawings to Palser, who had a shop near Astley's Theatre in the Westminster Road. In this occupation he met Samuel Prout with whom he made a friendly agreement not to exhibit at the same shop at the same time.

The works by other artists which Cox saw in the dealers' windows made him dissatisfied with his own comparatively untutored efforts, and he was determined to spend some of his exiguous resources on lessons, thereby showing a practical sense and strength of will which were to mark his character throughout his life. He debated whether he should apply to John Varley, John Glover or William Havell, but a chance meeting with Varley at Palser's decided him upon the first alternative. Cox took a number of lessons from Varley at his studio near Golden Square, for which he paid ten shillings a lesson until Varley discovered that Cox was a professional artist, a fact which he had concealed with characteristic discretion. 'I hear you are an artist, Mr Cox,' said Varley. 'No Sir, I am only trying to be one,' was the very typical reply. After that Varley, who was usually

2B KENILWORTH CASTLE   (WATER-COLOUR)   LADY LEVER ART GALLERY, PORT SUNLIGHT

in need of money, refused to accept any further fee, but gave Cox a free invitation to come and watch him at work whenever he felt inclined to do so. A romantic landscape 'Evening', p. 53 (No. 1917/135) in the City Art Gallery, Manchester, reveals strongly the influence of Varley, together with that of Girtin, with whom Varley had worked at the house of Dr Monro, who employed artists to copy from his collection of drawings in return for a small sum and their supper. Another water-colour, which probably dates from this first London period, is 'A Watermill in North Wales' (No. 3028/1876) in the Victoria and Albert Museum: this peaceful country scene, with ducks swimming on a village pond, has distinct affinities with John Varley. The paint is thinly laid on, and in places the pencil or charcoal outlines are clearly seen, a feature evident in many of Cox's compositions.

3 OLD WESTMINSTER   (WATER-COLOUR)   BIRMINGHAM ART GALLERY

4 OLD HOUSES AT HEREFORD    (WATER-COLOUR)    BIRMINGHAM ART GALLERY

Very early in his career Cox was encouraged by having two drawings accepted by the Royal Academy. The exhibition of 1805 contained a 'Kenilworth Castle' and a 'View on the River Mersey', which were probably elaborated versions of sketches made whilst Cox was touring with Macready's theatrical company. Cox exhibited each year until 1808, after which he ceased until 1827.*

It is indeed surprising that Cox gave up exhibiting at the Academy when that institution was still enjoying the reflected glamour of its first President, Reynolds, and an inclusion in its list of members was a hall-mark to success; but Cox as well as being unworldly was always primarily a water-colour painter and preferred to show his work in

*Cox exhibited but rarely at the Royal Academy; the Academy records account for only twelve pictures in all, nine being exhibited by 1829 and the remaining three in the years 1843 and 1844. In an interleaved catalogue, now in the Royal Academy Library, James Hughes Anderton noted the following comment regarding No. 296 in the exhibition of 1844 'Going to the Hayfield': 'Given his subject, who could better execute it, for you might see the grass in the process of drying into hay.'

exhibitions which specialized in his own medium, particularly the Society of Artists in Water-colour. This famous Society, which now has its headquarters in Conduit Street, opened in April 1805, at number 20 Lower Brook Street in premises which had formerly belonged to the Flemish dealer, Gerard Vandergucht. Among the sixteen foundation members were the brothers Varley, William Havell, Francis Nicholson, Joshua Cristall, Robert Hills and George Barret, and all submitted works to the opening exhibition, at which the scheme of placing an attendant in the rooms, with a price-list of the paintings and a register of the purchasers' names, was tried as an innovation. The exhibition succeeded beyond the most optimistic expectation of the organizers. Connoisseurs and leaders of fashion flocked to see it and in seven weeks nearly 12,000 persons paid for admission. The effect was so encouraging that the Secretary, on the closing of the exhibition, thanked the critics and public for their support and announced that the exhibition would be an annual event. The press dealt kindly with the water-colour artists; in fact the *Morning Post* published reviews longer and more favourable than those on the Royal Academy, which undoubtedly suffered from its rivalry with the Society. The *St James's Chronicle*, for instance, in reviewing the Academy exhibition of 1807 attributed the decline of interest in the water-colours at Somerset House to the fact that the most skilled exponents of the medium were very naturally exhibiting in their own Gallery.

Difficulties of accommodation and increasing membership obliged the Society to make frequent changes of address which is apt to lead to confusion in references to works exhibited under their auspices. In 1807 the Society removed to more convenient rooms, leased by Mr Christie the auctioneer, at 118 Pall Mall (near Carlton House), and the following year they went to 16 Old Bond Street at which premises they figured in Ackermann's *Microcosm of London* (Vol. II, pl. 34). Ackerman's illustrators, Pugin and Rowlandson, represented the water-colour exhibition as a smart but not overcrowded

5 'DOMESTICK DUCKS'    ILLUSTRATION IN AQUATINT FROM 'THE ARTIST'S COMPANION'

event; the public attracted thither appear to be the elegant intelli-
gentsia, and they are taking an active interest in the pictures, which
are hung in the jig-saw style accepted as the convention for art
galleries until comparatively recently. It is noticeable that the water-
colours are mostly very large, which indicates that the painters were
trying to match for exhibition purposes the average oil painting.
Ackermann in the text refers to the advantage of this exhibition over
the water-colours as shown at Somerset House, where the 'best room
is solely appropriated for pictures in oil'; and the water-colours with
less important oils are relegated to smaller rooms in which 'they,
whose beauty is derived from a minute attention to parts . . . must
suffer considerably . . . when opposed to half an acre of canvas
covered with the strongest tints'.

C                                    *33*

In 1809 the Water-colour Society found a home in Spring Gardens where they remained until 1820. After a short period in the Egyptian Hall, Piccadilly, they obtained, in 1823, premises at No. 5 Pall Mall East, which was known as the Gallery of the Society of Painters in Water-colour and where they entered on a period of increasing prosperity. Cox joined the Society in 1812 and between the following year until his death in 1859 he exhibited no less than eight hundred and forty-nine paintings in their rooms.

In 1805 Cox made his first journey to North Wales, where he is thought to have been joined by Charles Barber; and this tour through the romantic scenery of Merioneth and Caernarvonshire fired him with his constant love for the Welsh landscape. For some sketches, made in Wales the following year, he took with him a few water-colours which he had ready dissolved in bottles. A favourite method too was drawing in chalk on blue paper which he practised at intervals throughout his career. He continued occasionally to fulfil commissions for painting scenery; and it is recorded that one midsummer a certain Mr Hills, a builder who had married Mrs Ragg's second daughter, rigged up some rough equipment in his builder's yard so that Cox could complete some scenery which had to be done in distemper in a great hurry before the rains of autumn fell.

Cox's marriage in 1808 was the beginning of domestic happiness. Mary seems to have been the ideal wife for him. Some eight years older than David, she brought to bear upon his mind a mature influence for good; and she possessed a discriminating taste, especially in literature. It was customary for Mary Cox to read aloud to David, whilst he worked, from biographies, books of travel and occasionally a novel. She herself drew a little and David valued her opinion upon his work. Her only failing was her health: Mary was always delicate, and her son would say that his first memory of his mother was a 'pale lady who could just walk round the garden'. Shortly after the marriage the couple moved to Dulwich Common, where David Cox junior was born in the summer of 1809. Dulwich Common was then a wild and lonely place, frequented by gypsies who encamped in the woods belonging to the College. Cox made studies of these people, of their donkeys, caravans and trappings, which served him as notes for 'incidents' in his compositions in later life. However, his reaction towards his picturesque neighbours was not always one of unmixed aesthetic pleasure: at times these gypsies could be dangerous and Cox would relate how, one night when crossing the Common with his pockets filled with provisions, he saw a man lying in wait for him. He ran home by a different route with packets of sugar beating against his sides. Soon after the baby's birth Cox took the family for a holiday to his parents, who had now moved into the centre of Birmingham (near the corner of Hill Street and Swallow Street). There he divided his time between giving lessons, sketching in the suburbs, and minding the baby. Nearly every year whilst he lived in London Cox visited his parents in Birmingham. In a sketch-book of rough blue paper, which he used during his stay in 1810, he made studies of old buildings in and near the city and sketched Kenilworth Castle and scenes down a mine in Dudley.

In common with most artists of his time David Cox had to make his living by teaching, which was always irksome to him. Fortunately, there was a constant demand for drawing-masters, as the early part of the nineteenth century was an era when the social equipment of a young lady had to include an ample list of accomplishments of which sketching was one of the most important. The streets where successful artists lived are said to have been crowded with the carriages of the quality who would pay a guinea an hour to watch the painting of a picture by an artist of the most fashionable repute. Some contemporary notes by a kinsman of the water-colour painter Francis Nicholson (1753–1844), published in the *Old Water-colour Society's Club* (Vol. VIII, pp. 10, 11), describe the rage for water-colours which followed the opening exhibition in 1805. 'For some years after the doorsteps of artists were beset (by applicants for lessons). . . . It became an absolute craze among Ladies of Fashion to profess landscape painting.

To such a degree was this mania carried that every hour of the day was devoted to this easy employment and the more difficulty there was found in obtaining admission the greater of course became the anxiety to gain it. No time was too early, no hour too late for receiving what was called a lesson.' One lady, who applied for lessons from Nicholson, was told that the only hour vacant was 'eight o'clock in the morning, twice a week'; and, nothing daunted, she would sally forth to the studio in an elegant 'deshabille nightcap and with hair *en papillottes*' and after an hour's tuition return home to bed. Another indication of the more ludicrous aspect of the enthusiasm for drawing occurs in a skit, written toward the end of the eighteenth century when a servant is given orders not to admit any visitors to interrupt the artistic activities of his mistress: 'If anyone calls, say I can't be seen; I'm skying.'

A famous conversation in *Pride and Prejudice* reveals that Jane Austen was aware of how exacting and absurd were these social obligations of a lady. Elizabeth is at Netherfield and talking with the Bingleys about the qualifications for an accomplished woman. Charles Bingley would limit it to painting tables, covering screens and netting purses; but Miss Bingley, with feminine scorn, declares that 'no-one can be really esteemed accomplished, who does not greatly surpass what is usually met with. A woman must have a thorough knowledge of music, singing, drawing, dancing and the modern languages, to deserve the word.' Sometimes the drawing classes were so large that the object for copy had to be viewed by some of the pupils through a mirror; and this excessive popularity did harm to painters as well as to pupils. Teaching could become very lucrative to the unscrupulous, and masters could easily be as slap-dash as their protegés were un-critical. Painters who taught were obliged to devise a method by which to simplify their art, and it was only the more independent spirits who could resist a formula. A common procedure was for the painter to put in all the modelling and shading in monochrome, before adding the colouring in flat washes. By this method even the moderately accomplished pupil could achieve some success, whereas he, or more likely she, would have been led astray by Turner's unconventional technical devices. Text-books on sketching were profuse, and many were written by the artists themselves. Samuel Prout wrote several handbooks, one of which was naïvely entitled *Bits for Beginners*, and Cox's constant analysis of his own method and experience as a teacher resulted in his publication of his *Treatise on Landscape Painting* and other essays on technique. As has been seen, a normal method of making money for impecunious artists was to sell their drawings for copying; and John Sell Cotman, who suffered bitterly under the yoke of teaching, would hire out his drawings for this purpose.

Whilst at Dulwich Cox's name was drawn for the militia, but his distaste for military occupations and reluctance to waste time which could profitably have been employed in painting caused him to make representations to headquarters for release. When these were unsuccessful he offered to pay for a substitute, but in this also he was refused; and he had to leave home for a time for fear of being arrested as a deserter. On his return his fortunes sank very low, and in desperation he put up a notice in his window 'Perspective Taught Here'. In order to give some backing to his purely instinctive knowledge of the science, Cox bought a book of Euclid. Geometry, however, was not his *forte*, and enraged by the complexity of the propositions he flung the book away with such force that it shot through the wall, which was made of lath and plaster, and disappeared inside the battens. By a strange coincidence his first pupil was a small builder; and one would like to think that he repaid his master by repairing the damage. Greater profit came to Cox from Palser's shop where Colonel the Hon. Henry Windsor, afterwards the Earl of Plymouth, saw his drawings and enquired for particulars of lessons. Fortunately, Dulwich was on the way to the Colonel's home at Beckenham, and so Cox acquired his first patron. At the opening lesson Cox's pupil was so absorbed in his work that he did not (or refused to) notice that his master's dinner of a roast chicken was being burnt to a cinder. This

*37*

lack of consideration was, however, a triviality compared to the bene-
fits conferred on Cox by Windsor who introduced and recommended
him as a master to a distinguished social circle, including ladies in
high position such as Lady Arden, Lady Gordon, Lady Sophia
Cecil, Lady Burrell, the Hon. Misses Eden and Miss Tylney Long.
His terms were at first five shillings for an hour's lesson but, on the
advice of Colonel Windsor's mother, he raised them to ten-and-six.

In 1809 Cox began exhibiting with the Associated Artists in
Water-colour, founded in 1807, but which did not long outlive its
rivalry with the Society of Painters in Water-colour. Cox became
President in 1810 but reverted to being an associated member in the
following year. The demise of the Association in June 1812 cost Cox
dearly when he had little to lose on exhibition expenses. One of the
paintings he there exhibited was a large view of Windsor Castle which
years later was found to be backed by two other drawings, so little
did he prize his work or expect others to do so. In 1812, the year when
he began his treatise, Cox was elected as an associate, and in December a full member, of the Water-colour Society.

Earning a livelihood was still an uphill grind for Cox, and the
highest price he seems to have obtained for a single picture between
the years 1811 and 1814 was five pounds. Among his purchasers were
several citizens of Birmingham, including a friend, Mr Allen Everitt,
who kept a shop for art materials in Union Street where his son
Edward was one of Cox's earliest pupils, and Mr W. Radclyffe, the
engraver. Signs that the publishers of engravings, the middlemen of
art production, were beginning to notice Cox are indicated in the fact
that Ackermann's *Drawing-Book of Light and Shadow in Imitation
of Indian Ink*, published in 1812, contains some plates after Cox,
aquatinted by Sutherland and Bluck as early as 1809 and 1810.
Cox was represented, too, in Hassell's *Aqua Pictura*, produced during
the period 1813-1818 which included reproductions of work by
Girtin, Turner and de Loutherbourg. This encouragement could not,
however, have been such as to turn Cox's head, for in 1812, in

addition to receiving three guineas each for twenty-four copper-plates, it is recorded that he was paid five shillings for colouring four sporting prints. In 1816 Messrs S. and J. Fuller paid Cox £63 for twenty-four copper-plates at the rate of £2 12s. 6d. each.

In the spring of 1812 Cox went to Hastings (a resort then much frequented by painters) where he did many drawings of fishing-boats and fisher-people, in company with the painter Havell. Here Cox tried his hand at oil painting, and among the results may have been the small works now at Birmingham: 'All Saints' Church, Hastings' (No. 2509/85), Frontispiece, and 'Fishing Boats at Hastings' (No. 2486/85). These are some of Cox's most successful achievements in oil, although far less ambitious than his work done when he seriously studied this medium. They have a simplicity of designing and a breadth of colour massing which make them comparable with Constable's oil sketches. A sepia study of 'All Saints' Church' is engraved in aquatint in Cox's 'Treatise' as the upper portion of plate XXXVI. Cox indeed was influenced by Constable as were most landscape painters of his time, but he appears to have made no specific reference to his debt to the greater master in his notes and correspondence.

In spite of exhibiting at the Water-colour Society and occasionally elsewhere,* Cox does not appear yet to have found a ready market for his drawings. The times were unfavourable to a young artist who had no 'name' with which to attract purchasers who were feeling the effects of trade depression caused by the wars with France. Often in despair he would destroy his work, and in later years he would show his friends a grating near the Thames down which he would throw away his drawings. Economic necessity obliged him to combine two activities which he disliked, soldiering and teaching, by accepting, in 1813, a post as drawing master at the Military College at Farnham. This necessitated a move from his cottage at Dulwich and, during Cox's absence at Farnham, his wife went to her mother at Camber-

* Only three works by Cox are recorded as having been exhibited at the British Institution in 1814, 1828, and 1843 respectively.

6A ST MARY'S CHURCH AND COUNTY HALL, WARWICK   (WATER-COLOUR)   BIRMINGHAM ART GALLERY

well, and the boy divided his time between his grandparents in Birmingham and his aunt in Lancashire.

At Farnham Cox was given the honorary rank of Captain, with a batman to wait on him, and he enjoyed the company of some of the senior officers; but the atmosphere of militarism was foreign to his easy-going temperament, and he disliked the accurate map-drawing which he had to master as well as the discipline to which he, like the others, was subjected. For instance before going to London he had to ask permission. Furthermore, his exacting work as teacher prevented him from pressing forward as an artist, and in 1815 he did not send to the Water-colour Society exhibition. The Governor of the College and members of his staff made allowances for the special position of the painter, and with mutual goodwill Cox was released

*40*

6B HIGH STREET MARKET, BIRMINGHAM  ENGRAVING FROM 'GRAPHIC ILLUSTRATIONS OF WARWICKSHIRE'

from his duties after the first term or two, and returned to his wife at Camberwell.

His troubles, however, were not over, and his obligations towards his family necessitated his taking another post as teacher: a form of employment not likely to be hard to obtain as every English town of any size had its drawing master, and in some fashionable centres such as Bath they abounded. An advertisement in *The Times* informed Cox that a reliable instructor was needed in a school for young ladies at Hereford under the direction of Miss Croucher who offered £100 a year for teaching in the school twice a week, thereby affording opportunity to the successful candidate to take private pupils. Cox accepted the post, which appealed to him not only on economic grounds but because it enabled him to live and work near his beloved North Wales.

Furthermore young David would receive good education at the Hereford Grammar School. His departure from London was marked by expressions of goodwill and regret among his pupils. Lady Arden defrayed the cost of his removal by the loan of £40 which he repaid with a picture, and the Ladies Exeter and Sophia Cecil wished him and his family good fortune in their new life and asked for 'his direction in Herefordshire' so that they should be able to keep in touch at least by correspondence.

The work done by Cox during the period which closed with his removal to Herefordshire promised tasteful competence, but hardly the bold excellence of his maturity. Few would then have prognosticated his rank among the famous water-colour painters of his generation, although the discerning might have seen in some of his early water-colours careful planning, a sensitive use of flat masses, giving an effect of solidity, and a firm if gentle handling of colour; qualities also noticeable in the very charming early oils. The effect of the sound grounding with the Barbers is apparent, but Cox shows an independence of judgment missing from the agreeable mediocrity which characterizes the work of Joseph Barber and his sons. The Birmingham Collection contains several sketches in water-colour, pen and wash by all three Barbers, mostly representing local views and architectural subjects; they are pleasant records but none bears any real distinction. In this so-called 'first period', Cox used a restricted palette, the main colours being lake, gamboge, indigo and sepia.

The most important event in Cox's artistic life up to this time was the publication in 1813–14 by Messrs S. and J. Fuller at the Temple of Fancy, Rathbone Place, Oxford Street, of his *Treatise on Landscape Painting and Effect in Water-colours*, where he laid down rules and principles to which in the main he adhered throughout his life. The book was undertaken at the 'urgent and repeated solicitations of many of his pupils' who asked for guidance in the 'selection of appropriate effects of Nature adapted to the different characters of

42

landscape composition'; and the essence of his counsel is to approach Nature carefully, and not to falsify her effects. According to Cox 'the principal art of Landscape Painting consists in conveying to the mind the most forcible effect which can be produced from the various classes of scenery; which possesses the power of exciting an interest superior to that resulting from any other effect; and which can only be obtained by a judicious selection of particular tints, and a skilful arrangement and application of them to differences in time, seasons and situation.'

The text of the *Treatise* is wordy (it is rumoured that in writing it Cox was helped anonymously by a clergyman who may have been better intentioned than he was literary) but some of Cox's advice is very sound: he impresses the pupil with the necessity of becoming 'thoroughly acquainted with, and of obtaining a proper feeling of, the subject' and urges that 'the picture should be complete and perfect in the mind before it is even traced upon the canvas'. No muddled thinking, much careful planning and an ordered simplicity of outlook: all are excellent objectives for any young artist. Unity of composition, too, he recommends: 'the student should ever keep in view the principal object which induced him to make the sketch . . . and the prominence of this leading feature in the piece should be duly supported throughout, every other subject introduced should be sub-servient to it, and the attraction of the one should be the attraction of the whole.' Cox attached especial importance to tone values. 'All lights in a picture should be composed of warm tints', he exhorts, 'except they fall on a glossy or reflective surface; such as laurel leaves, glazed utensils, etc., which should be cool, and the lights small to give them a sparkling appearance . . . the opposition of a cool to a warm colour assists greatly in giving brilliancy to the lights. If a picture, for instance, should have a cool sky, the landscape ought to be principally composed of warm tints. . . .' Cox's early training with Barber is implicit in his remarks about accuracy of draughtsmanship: 'he who devotes his time to the completion of a perfect outline . . . has more than half finished his piece; while the author of a slovenly outline creates for himself an infinity of trouble. Where the pupil has made a correct and decided outline, all timidity vanishes.' The student is advised to attain proficiency in the 'art of pencilling . . .' By 'practising drawing from casts of the antique . . . he will also find his progress accelerated by the dedication of his leisure moments to copying objects of still life—a practice which will be found replete with advantage, when he studies combinations of subjects for compositions of landscape scenery. . . .' The refinements of a picture in Cox's view are achieved by the adroit management of light and shade. 'It is here that the Art begins to display its varied and inexhaustible beauties. . . . Light and Shade should be studied in sepia or Indian ink . . . the variety of colour tending to perplex the mind. . . . Colouring is a distinct and subsequent branch and is only to be learnt by long and minute observation of the diversified tints and hues of Nature. The principle of Light and Shade is established by theory.' Cox's remarks on technique are interesting. He recommends his pupil to mix three or four carefully matched shades according to the number of distances there may be in the subject, and to work forward from the third distance. He should then lay in all the shades or masses of shadow, which should be modified by small touches of a lighter tint 'as in fractured stone, brick or broken plaster', or deepened accents of shadow. Cox insists on the value of a full brush. 'The pencil should be full of colour in order that it may float.'

In the rules regarding effect Cox does appear somewhat dated and dogmatic, and it is hard to believe in many contemporary artists falling in with his dicta that 'a flat country . . . a winding river . . . should be seen beneath a grey, clouded sky . . . the old Pollard Willow is strictly characteristic . . . a Cottage or Village requires a soft and simple admixture of tones . . . the structures of greatness and antiquity should be marked by a character of awful sublimity . . .' and so on in the romantic vein typical of early nineteenth century taste.

The book was illustrated with a number of plates, many of them in colour and accompanied by explicit colour notes. These plates, Cox enjoined, should 'be copied in regular succession and any bad line . . . should be entirely expunged'. The drawings reproduced range from single elements of composition, such as still-life studies, eggs and a bowl, cottages, bridges, a dove-cote and pump, windmills, boats and individual trees to elaborate landscapes. The notes attached to the plates in colour show the restricted palette with which Cox achieved the effects that he advised his students to copy. For instance Cox tells that 'Wind', of which the water-colour, now in the British Museum and known as 'A Windmill, Herefordshire', and engraved by Reeve as plate LXIII, was executed in indigo, Indian red, van Dyck brown, burnt sienna and clear touches of lake.

The Treatise is hardly a very stimulating work, but it is indeed a revealing portrait of its author. It contains nothing startlingly original, nothing violent or rebellious: all is sound, kindly, common-sense advice. The soul of the man is expressed through its pages: one who believed in careful craftsmanship, who loved nature in all her various moods; and who understood the English countryside so intimately and with such humility that his friends would call him 'Farmer Cox'.

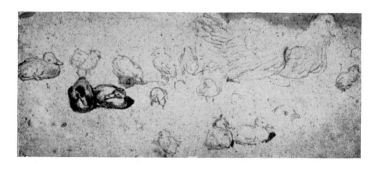

*Study of ducks*

*Study of drapery*

# III
# HEREFORD
## *1814-1827*

TOWARDS THE END OF 1814 THE COX FAMILY ARRIVED AT the ancient cathedral city which was to be their home for the next twelve years. The romantic flavour of the place, with its mixture of noble old buildings and pleasant country views, must have appealed to the artist to whom some link with natural beauties was essential to modify his distaste for urban life. When oppressed by the monotony of a school curriculum he could wander through the meadows beside the river Wye, or, if material cares belaboured him almost past the point of bearing, he could gaze upon the cathedral as a symbol of the Eternal which renders trivial the ephemeral perplexities of Man.

Cox's first home at Hereford was a cottage at Lower Lyde, near Ailstone Hill; a primitive place containing only the barest necessities of living. The winter in this desolate spot must have been an ordeal for them all; and at the earliest opportunity (in the spring of 1815) Cox removed to a more convenient house called George Cottage, near Baynton Wood on the North side of the hill.* As Cox's fortunes improved so his standard of comfort was raised; in 1817 he went to a picturesque cottage in Parry's Lane where he built a studio, with the financial assistance of his landlord, Mr Parry, who held a sympathetic opinion of artists and allowed Cox £40 towards the additions, leaving the planning to him. Mr Parry did not even

---

* This cottage was burnt down on 28 April, 1923.

47

increase the rent, which was £80 a year; and for a sum of some thirty pounds, drawn from his own purse, David Cox built a studio with a living-room combined, and a bedroom above it. The garden, where he grew hollyhocks, one of his favourite flowers, contained an old well where Mrs Cox used to hang the meat which was stolen on one occasion shortly before she was due to receive some guests for dinner.

David Cox remained at Parry's Lane for some six and a half years, until he built Ash Tree House on a plot of land he had purchased on the brow of Ailstone Hill. This was evidently a grander residence than its predecessor, as it was approached by a circular carriage drive. Moreover its amenities were such as to appeal to a West Indian merchant, one Reynolds, who bought it from Cox in 1827 and renamed it Berbice Villa. Mr Reynolds certainly showed an astute business sense in his handling of the transaction, as instead of a few shillings change he requested the artist to present him with 'five or six little drawings for the balance'.

Cox began his classes at Miss Croucher's Academy of Drawing for girls on October 26 1814, and continued to teach there until the end of 1819. It was a boarding school of some repute, and was housed in a picturesque half-timbered building in Widemarsh Street. Cox's work there was uninspiring, as he had to instruct somewhat dreary girls in a type of draughtsmanship which appealed little to him, such as the more academic kind of figure drawing and still-life compositions. A large group of flowers in water-colour in the Birmingham Collection (No. 98/35), is a reflection of the duties which Cox as drawing-master had to perform. In addition to Miss Croucher's girls Cox also took classes at the Grammar School (for the annual fee of six guineas) and taught the pupils of a Miss Poole, who paid him fifteen guineas for half a year's instruction to five of her young ladies. Teaching elegant accomplishments to the Herefordians was a drudgery for Cox. He sometimes had to be escorted to his pupil's house by his insistent wife who would not give in to his protestations of disinclination, nor was it by any means adequately remunerative, for Cox was obliged further to tax his energies by travelling round the countryside to estates of the landed gentry and by teaching in schools at Leominster and other market-towns. To ease these journeys Cox bought a pony but he found equitation a greater strain even than teaching, and after numerous mishaps he reverted to walking! The Misses Hopton, daughters of the Vicar of Canon Frome, William Turton, the son of the agent of the Duke of Beaufort, J. M. Ince, the artist, and the family of the Rev J. Lelly (for whom Cox made a drawing of their home, New Court, which was reproduced in lithograph by Hullmandel), were among his more notable private pupils whose fees ranged from 7s. 6d. to 10s. 6d. a lesson. In one of his notebooks it appears that Cox received at the rate of seventy pounds a year for some of his pupils and seventy guineas for others in respect of board, lodging and instruction.

Cox's first-hand knowledge of the difficulties of making a living encouraged his advanced Liberal opinions, which led to his being appointed to the Committee formed to welcome Joseph Hume, the political reformer, on his visit to Hereford in 1820. With two others Cox subscribed to present Hume with a hogshead of good Hereford-shire cider, and in his honour he attended an official dinner, thus making one of his very few appearances at a public function. To commemorate the ceremony he planted some oak trees in his garden. When stirred by the deepest convictions Cox could abandon his normal conformity to convention for the hazards of an independent outlook. The same spirit which had induced him to defy the call-up to the militia encouraged Cox to take the side of the unpretending in any political argument. On many such occasions, indeed, his wife had to keep the peace. Cox resented deeply the imposition of certain taxes, and took a childish pleasure in depriving the revenue of dues by drinking substitutes for tea, such as a certain kind of roasted corn which he much disliked. On one occasion he experimented in making an infusion from new-mown hay! Cox's radical views, however, mellowed as he grew older, and in his later years he seems to have taken very little interest in politics.

The drawings made by Cox in his first years at Hereford are usually reticent in tone, with the colour laid on in flat pale washes. The 'Old Houses at Hereford', p. 31 (No. 331/07) at Birmingham, is a charming example of Cox's manner in water-colour when he was emerging from the tentative style of his youth into the more decisive technique of his so-called 'second period', which covers his years of residence at Hereford. In this drawing the palette is still restricted to a few low tones, but there is a weight of accomplishment in the draughtsmanship (note the firm handling of the stone bridge) which shows an advance in maturity from the delicate 'Old Westminster' done some ten years before. Another example at Birmingham, 'Old Houses at Kenilworth' (No. 380/07), in Indian ink and wash, displays Cox's already assured treatment of an architectural subject.

The unobtrusive tones and pleasant washes of these early drawings were to give place to a more precise technique, which satisfied the misconception of the public that an artist and a drawing-master were necessarily identical. The vogue of the topographical picture, continued from the eighteenth century, combined with a popular demand for realistic painting, developed a taste for landscape scenes which were the forerunners of the photograph. A water-colour at Birmingham representing 'Buckingham House from the Green Park' (No. 68/11), facing p. 16, dated 1825, shows how successfully Cox could produce a painting which had all the qualities necessary to make it easily saleable. It is bright in colouring, minute in brushwork and 'easy on the eye'; but its charm is one of subject rather than treatment, and its chic appearance is far removed from the rugged sincerity of Cox's most characteristic work. Historically the drawing is interesting, as it shows the red brick residence of George III shortly before it was reconstructed in the Palladian style.

Whilst at Hereford Cox produced a number of works which were frankly topographical and intended for publication in books of views; also he added to his text books. *Progressive Lessons in Landscape for Young Beginners*, published by Fuller in 1816, contained some very simple soft-ground etchings by Cox; and in 1817 he drew six views of Bath, which were aquatinted by Smart and Sutherland and published by Fuller in 1820. Cox received twenty-four guineas for making these records of the city of crescents and promenades. The *Treatise* was followed by *The Young Artist's Companion*, also embellished by plates in outline, sepia and in colours. The *Companion* was published by S. and J. Fuller between October 1819 and January 1821 in sixteen monthly numbers mostly at *2s. 6d.* each, the three last, in colours, being priced at *5s*.

A feature of the *Companion* was, in addition to forty soft-ground etchings and twelve aquatints in imitation of sepia, its striking colour-plates, made in aquatint by Reeve, and including some unusual still-life studies such as some mackerel, a harvester's luncheon basket and a group of bottles, for use in foregrounds. An attractive plate in colour is called 'Domestick Ducks', p. 33: birds which evidently caught the fancy of Cox who made numerous studies of their movements and plumage. A water-colour sketch for the plate representing a basket with foxgloves, clothes and other objects, inscribed 'D. Cox, Hereford', is in the Birmingham Gallery (No. 36/31). Especially interesting is the frontispiece showing an arrangement of the artist's own drawings, both finished and unfinished. The text, arranged in a series of progressive lessons, follows the *Treatise* in principle, and often *verbatim*. Cox again pays particular attention to the effect given to each scene. 'Abrupt and irregular lines are productive of a grand or stormy effect, whilst serenity is the result of even and horizontal lines. Morning effect may be displayed in any composition . . . owing to the great glare of light in mid-day effects, hayfields, cornfields or any busy scene on rivers are suitable . . . as regards evening and twilight, such effects being calculated to convey to the mind impressions of grandeur, the composition should be studied to produce the same, and the colouring ought to be perfectly in unison with the

51

peaceful repose or the gloomy majesty which contrasts the scene.'

A sense of the appropriate is a virtue which Cox is ever anxious to instil into his pupils. 'All objects which are not in character with the scenes should be carefully avoided, as the introduction of any unnecessary object is sure to be attended with injurious consequences.' Also he urges sincerity of purpose in the painter who should not regard his work simply as an exposition of talent. 'Merely to paint is not enough' he affirmed. Cox's injunctions on outline, light and shade and on colouring contain elements of wisdom which could well be followed by young painters of any period and he warns against any form of slackness either in idea or method. 'A picture should be complete in the mind before it is even traced upon the canvas,' is a remark which illustrates the importance Cox placed upon clear thinking. His references to the necessity of having a number of saucers 'to mix each separate shade in' and the paper 'strained upon a proper drawing board' show how neatly he attended to detail.

As well as Messrs Fuller, T. Clay of Ludgate Hill commissioned Cox to work for their educational publications. *A Series of Progressive Lessons intended to elucidate the Art of Landscape Painting in Water-colours*, ran through several editions between 1811 and 1828. Some of the later issues contained lithographs by Day and aquatints by Hunt after David Cox. Messrs. Ackermann seem to have taken over this publication and varied it. A reprint issued by them in 1841 has plates by David Cox junior whilst a subsequent edition of 1845 contains plates after Cox father and son.

In 1829 appeared *Graphic Illustrations of Warwickshire* with line engravings by Radclyffe of Birmingham after de Wint, J. V. Barber, David Cox and others with letterpress by Dr Alexander Blair. Cox's six contributions were made in 1826 and 1827, shortly before he left Hereford for London. The original drawings are in the Birmingham Gallery. All but one are in sepia, the exception being the well-known water-colour 'St Mary's Church and the County Hall, Warwick', p. 40,

7A EVENING   (WATER-COLOUR)   CITY ART GALLERY, MANCHESTER

(No. P.L.22) which is rather steely in colouring and tight in texture, but has a vivacity of draughtsmanship (particularly in the figures) which retrieves it from the banal. Two of the series 'High Street Market, Birmingham', p. 41 (No. P.L.19) and 'Guy's Cliff from the Avenue' (No. P.L.23), were sent to Radclyffe for engraving a few days before Cox left Hereford and the latter was a free gift to the publishers (for the other drawings Cox received one guinea each).

For his engraving of the High Street Cox used all the resources of his ingenuity. The scene is one of bustling animation; a market is in progress for the sale of live geese and dead hares, and street vendors are plying their trade. The view is down the High Street, looking across the Bull Ring to Saint Martin's Church, with Saint John's Church, Deritend, in the middle distance and Trinity Chapel,

Bordesley, on the sky-line. When forwarding the drawing to the engraver Cox expressed some misgivings. 'I have this moment recollected that I ought to have made a sketch of some ducks,' he wrote 'but I think if it is to be altered you can do it, and I will touch up on the proof. I still think there can be no objection to the table with the dead poultry.'

During these years at Hereford, David Cox made various journeys, making sketches wherever he went. In 1816 he travelled down the Wye to Chepstow, which resulted in seven drawings at the current Exhibition at the Water-colour Society. The following year he was seriously ill and sent nothing to London, but in 1818 he travelled to North Wales, and in 1819 to Devon and again to Bath—this last journey being impressed on his memory as 'very dull' because he was

7B CLASSICAL COMPOSITION   (WATER-COLOUR)   VICTORIA AND ALBERT MUSEUM

alone. '*Voyager seul, c'est le plus triste de nos plaisirs*' would have been the opinion of David Cox, who always tried to take with him companions even if they were bent on amusement rather than on art.

Almost every year on his way to London Cox would pass through Birmingham where he would sell some drawings and enjoy the company of his friends, notably the Everitts. In 1819 he took his son with him to London when they visited the exhibitions, and are said to have been much impressed by a painting by Wilkie of 'Chelsea Pensioners'.* The picturesque dress and setting of the Pensioners' Hospital evidently attracted Cox, as he used the subject for a water-colour, which was exhibited at the Fine Art Society, June 1946 (No. 6). In London Cox would always try to visit Turner at his Gallery in Queen Anne Street where, for some reason unexplained, Cox would be greeted by the name of Daniel. On his return from one of these journeys Cox expressed his admiration for Turner in a drawing representing 'Aeneas approaching Carthage', which he appears to have repeated in various versions. A painting by Turner which Cox especially admired was the 'Harvest Dinner at Kingston Bank', now in the Tate Gallery. On one occasion when attempting to describe its beauty to Lady Arden he seized the cover of a piece of music and made on it a sketch as a reminder of the picture.

Cox's connexion with Turner and his subjection to the still prevailing prestige of the classical tradition is perhaps reflected in the 'Classical Composition', p. 54, (No. 873-1892) (*c.*1825) in the Victoria and Albert Museum, where he has transgressed beyond the normal by painting an imaginary landscape with a Roman temple silhouetted against the glow of sunset. Another tribute to Turner was probably paid in Cox's water-colour of 'Sunset over Shakespeare's Cliff, Dover' (No. B.85) in the British Museum, dating from the Hereford period.

---

*This incident is referred to by Solly (p. 42). If correct, Wilkie's picture could hardly have been the finished version of the celebrated 'Chelsea Pensioners Reading the Gazette of the Battle of Waterloo' which was not completed until 1822, when it was shown at the Academy where it exceeded in popularity any other painting there exhibited, a rail having to be placed before it to save the picture from damage by the poke-bonnets of the ladies who pressed forward to examine its detail.

8A QUAY IN NORTHERN FRANCE (WATER-COLOUR) BIRMINGHAM ART GALLERY

The golden trellis flung by the setting sun across a turquoise sea is a motive which Cox may possibly have seen in the work of Claude Lorraine but was probably made aware of through his associations with Turner. Turner reciprocated a regard for David Cox, to whom he gave a drawing, 'A View of Dudley' which is now in the Art Gallery at Dudley. It is similar to a sepia drawing by Cox in the same Art Gallery.

Each year Cox continued to exhibit at the Water-colour Society where, in 1826, he showed twenty-two drawings. In the summer of this same year David Cox, incurably insular, was induced to take the first of his three journeys to the Continent in company with his brother-in-law, Mr Gardener, an agent for a firm at 163 Regent Street which sold Government Ordnance Maps, who was commissioned to see a map of the world lately published in Brussels. Cox left his wife in the care of Ann Fowler (who had joined their service in 1819 and remained as Cox's faithful friend and housekeeper after the death of Mrs Cox), but, for the sake of education, he took young

David with him. They travelled by boat and diligence to Brussels, where Cox made numerous sketches and visited Waterloo, still invested with the glamour of the victory. In Brussels Cox met the Hoptons of Canon Frome, who were travelling 'in style', and with them he visited places of interest in Belgium and Holland. During this time his brush was not idle; and the lovely drawing of 'Ghent' below, (No. M.W.I. 988) in the Whitworth Art Gallery, Manchester, with its delicate misty tones reminiscent of de Wint, is a record of this tour. The composition is reminiscent of the 'Old Westminster', with the church, seen as through a haze, rising above the neighbouring houses. The 'Continental Street Scene', p. 58 (No. 330/07), a water-colour in the Birmingham collection, is probably a view in Brussels, made during Cox's visit. It is a gay, fantastic composition, distinctly suggestive of Cox's training as a scene-painter.

8B GHENT   (WATER-COLOUR)   WHITWORTH ART GALLERY, MANCHESTER

9 CONTINENTAL STREET SCENE    (WATER-COLOUR)    BIRMINGHAM ART GALLERY

A journey abroad was for Cox a mixed pleasure, but this first experience broadened his outlook, and on his return to Hereford he felt in need of a change. Through the attraction of the opposites he was again drawn to London, where he felt that, among the leading members of his profession and near the wealthy patrons and collectors, he would make more money both as artist and teacher and establish a better position for young David, now about 18. Furthermore, whilst in Hereford, whither he had gone almost penniless, he had amassed by diligent toil at least a thousand pounds which would start him on a new phase of his career. The prosperous Mr Reynolds provided the solution to the problem of disposing of Ash Tree House, and alternative accommodation was soon found at No. 9 Foxley Road, Kennington Common, S.E. Once more Mrs Cox had to face the fact that being married to an artist is an insecure existence. With regrets at leaving their quiet country home tempered by the prospect of being near her own people, she packed up her belongings and returned to the City where, nearly twenty years before, she had found a husband for whom she probably dreamed of many things of more material profit than a place among the Immortals.

*'The Boscobel Oak'* : *sign for 'The Royal Oak Inn', Bettws-y-Coed*

Dear Sir

On looking at the date of your letter I am concerned it has remained so long unanswered being from home when it arrived and very unwell since my return will I hope be a sufficient apology. The first day I can go to town I will bring my sketches of Old Houses in Hereford. which I made with a view to publish in in lithography and to which I have many subscribers. Should

it suit you I have no objection to make drawings in sepia from any of them at five guineas each

I am Sir your truly

David Cox

Dec 19th /20.
Foxley Road Kennington.

10  AUTOGRAPH LETTER    ROYAL ACADEMY

60

# IV
# LONDON
## *1827-1841*

WITH HIS RETURN TO THE CAPITAL BEGAN THE MOST arduous and the most rewarding period of Cox's life, when he explored not only new regions in which to paint, but new methods with which to express himself. This 'third period' was the epoch during which Cox made his extensive journeys through Yorkshire, Derbyshire, Lancashire, the Lake District, Kent and North and South Wales, and paid his two further visits to the Continent. During this time, too, he constantly exhibited, and adopted the use of a special kind of rough paper which helped the atmospheric 'out-of-doors' effects at which he specially aimed. It was indeed a period of constant physical strain, for Cox's conscience as a craftsman did not allow him to relax his standards whilst his commitments both as painter and teacher increased with his reputation.

Cox's health at the time of his departure from Hereford was poor; he was fatigued by the worries of combining domestic ease with artistic integrity. In a letter dated December 19th, 1828, of which the original is in an interleaved catalogue in the Royal Academy library, Cox asks a now unknown recipient to forgive his delay in replying due to his being very unwell since his return. He answers his acquaintance—obviously a would-be purchaser—that at the first opportunity he will bring him sketches of old buildings in Hereford which he made with a view to engraving and from which he would make drawings in 'seppia . . . at five guineas each'.

The London to which Cox returned was a more flourishing place than the war-worried city he had left in the year before Waterloo. The victories over Napoleon had effects both good and bad on the state of the arts in England. Increased prosperity and a sense of security encouraged the public to spend money on pictures, but with the revival of national self-confidence and a wider distribution of wealth was developed a complacency, an 'I-know-nothing-about-art-but-I-like-what-I-know' attitude, which tempted even the most independent artists profitably to turn out 'dining-room' oils or 'drawing-room' water-colours for which only too ready a market was forming.

In a London season David Cox could now acquire as many pupils as he had time to teach (among them were the Hon. Miss Leveson Gower and the Countess of Verulam). Society was eager to purchase as well as to learn, and the fashion for ladies to have albums containing drawings by recognized artists benefited Cox, who would recount how, during lessons, he used (with some embarrassment as he disliked anything in the nature of 'showing-off') to illustrate his method by painting a water-colour which his pupil, or her parents, would be enchanted to buy for five or ten guineas. In fact these personal contacts were for Cox more profitable than exhibitions where his work would frequently remain unsold. In the Art Gallery at Dudley are several 'demonstration sketches' which Cox used to illustrate his lessons. One shows a simplified method of drawing foliage by a congeries of zigzag lines and another contains perspective diagrams and illustrations of composition. On occasions Cox would prepare his pupils for their tours abroad by painting imaginary sketches of countries he had not seen. For example he made a number of studies, with elaborate notes, of the Rhineland for the benefit of Miss Frances Carr, who was about to travel in Germany. In the Birmingham collection is a slight sketch of a rotunda in Rome (No. 721/27) obviously based on an engraving. Without being conceited Cox was too assured an artist not to realize that his best work was under-estimated by the public; and on one occasion in a mood of whimsical disappointment he, himself, affixed 'sold' labels to a number of exhibited pictures which no one had shown the perspicacity to buy! The broad, rough technique of which Cox was a master seemed to the uninstructed to lack 'finish': in fact it bewildered some of them as a new idiom in painting. Cox would take rather wicked pleasure in making fun of an old lady whose conversation he overheard at an exhibition. She was being wheeled in an invalid chair by a girl from whom she asked for particulars about the pictures. When before a painting by Copley Fielding she expressed rapture; but a drawing by David Cox she denounced as 'very curious' and begged her companion to move her on quickly.

After two years in London Cox again took a trip abroad, an adventure of duty rather than of pleasure. In June 1829 he and his

11 WINDSOR CASTLE    (SEPIA WASH)    VICTORIA AND ALBERT MUSEUM

son crossed from Dover to Calais whence they proceeded in a leisurely fashion to Paris, stopping on the way to sketch at Amiens and Beauvais. The water-colour 'A Street in Beauvais' (No. 826/29) in the Victoria and Albert Museum records this visit. At Calais, where Cox made notes for numerous sketches, including the 'Street Scene with Lighthouse' in the Tate Gallery (No. 4301), he met François-Louis Francia, who had studied water-colour painting with Girtin and whose chief claim to eminence is as being one of Bonington's first teachers. It may have been that the two artists talked of Bonington, and even that Francia showed Cox examples of Bonington's work, for certain paintings by Cox done at that time have an atmosphere reminiscent of that brilliant, short-lived genius. 'Calais Sands' (No. 289/25) at Birmingham is very close to Bonington, whose warm, romantic glow is also reflected in a 'Shore Scene with Shrimpers' (No. 833—1936) in the Victoria and Albert Museum.

In Paris Cox and his son encountered the engraver John Pye, who met Cox while having his shoes blacked in the Tuileries Gardens and did him the honours of the city. Among the places of interest to which Pye took Cox was a gaming-house to which Cox consented to go only on being persuaded that he should 'see everything once'. On coming out Cox slipped and sprained his ankle, and he attributed this mishap to his wrongfulness in penetrating such a disgraceful place of entertainment. This accident prevented Cox from fulfilling his intention of visiting the châteaux on the Loire, but it did not deter him from driving or hobbling round Paris, sketching (sometimes from a cab) the famous views and buildings and making notes which he worked up into pictures for subsequent exhibitions. Among the subjects he chose were the Louvre and Tuileries, the Palais de Justice, the rue Saint Honoré and the church of Saint Eustache, as well as the various bridges over the Seine. In the Louvre he made a small copy in water-colour, now in the Birmingham Art Gallery (No. 92/37) of Titian's 'Virgin with the Rabbit'. This picture which has been widely copied by painters, was formerly

III SUN, WIND AND RAIN (WATER-COLOUR) BIRMINGHAM ART GALLERY

12  LADY HOLDING A BABY AT THE FONT    (WATER-COLOUR)
LENT TO THE BIRMINGHAM ART GALLERY BY MR M. BROWN

13 PEASANT CHILDREN (WATER-COLOURS)
IN POSSESSION OF SIR ROBERT WITT, C.B.E.

in the collection of King Charles I. Cox also seems to have visited Rouen, where he made a beautiful drawing of the 'Tour de l'Horloge', now in the Travelling Trust of the National Art Collections Fund. Cox's ignorance of the language detracted from his pleasure whilst in France, where he cast a very English suspicion upon the food and the 'foreign' ways! His pencil served as his interpreter. Instead of asking for an egg he would draw one, and in order that the waiter should know how he wanted it cooked he would represent the shell as broken and colour the yolk yellow. His next, and last, visit to France was a short trip in 1832 when he visited the ports, notably Dieppe and Boulogne. At the latter place he saw a review in honour of the Emperor Louis-Philippe. There are various water-colours in the Birmingham Gallery which refer to these journeys. The 'Calais Pier' (No. 95/19) is a rather conventional study, obviously done for sale and worked up from a sketch. This subject was repeated several times by Cox, usually in water-colour but on occasion in oil. The Walker Art Gallery at Liverpool contains a striking oil painting of 'Calais Pier' in which the sea is painted with the sparkle and freedom expected of Bonington although the figures are as flat as if cut out of paper. 'A Quay in Northern France', p. 56 (No. 243/27) at Birmingham, is one of Cox's most delicate water-colours, effective mainly because of its lack of any conscious striving after effect.

On his return from the first visit to France, Cox took lodgings at Gravesend where his wife had relatives, and he could indulge his pleasure in sketching the Thames.

River scenes particularly attracted Cox who found congenial subjects at Windsor and Eton, which he used to visit from London. A well-known drawing at the British Museum represents 'The Brocas, Eton' (No. 1900/8/29/492) and in the Victoria and Albert Museum is a delightfully romantic nocturne of 'Windsor Castle', p. 63 (No. 16—1896), done in sepia wash and possibly intended for reproduction. Other slight sketches of scenes on the Thames, in the same medium, are among the Holliday bequest in the Tate Gallery. 'On the Thames, Battersea' (No. 2516/85) in the Birmingham Gallery is an interesting example in oil of a river scene, and has a reticence of tone and solidity of treatment which suggest that Cox may have been looking at the work of one of the Dutch painters of sailing ships. With marine subjects Cox was usually only partially successful. Some of his harbour scenes and studies of hulks, boats and fisherfolk have the charm of freshness ('Shrimpers' (No. 270/25) at Birmingham is a notable example); but his seascapes are generally conventional and lack the tang of the salt air, an atmospheric effect which Bonington could miraculously convey. 'The Humber at Hull' (No. 90 in the City Art Gallery, Manchester) is a competent sea-piece in water-colour but it has little distinction of perception; 'Rhyl Sands' (No. P30–1930) in the Victoria and Albert Museum is a pleasant little water-colour, very fresh and breezy; and the 'Old Landing Stage, Liverpool' (No. WH/3302) at the Lady Lever Art Gallery, Port Sunlight, conveys a sense of air and space within very small dimensions.

In 1830, Cox went to Yorkshire where he took such a liking for

14A  A FISHERMAN    (WATER-COLOUR)    BIRMINGHAM ART GALLERY

Bolton Abbey that he visited it repeatedly, and used it as a subject for a number of picturesque scenes in oil and water-colour, mainly intended for exhibitions. A very characteristic water-colour of Bolton Abbey is in the Lady Lever Art Gallery, Port Sunlight, and an imposing exhibition picture of the same subject in oils is in the Walker Art Gallery, Liverpool.

As Cox's position as an artist became more secure, if never excessively remunerative, he acquired a number of friends among artists and amateurs with whom he, with his gift for friendship, kept on excellent terms. Samuel Prout, John Sell Cotman, William Havell,

*68*

14B TWO FARMERS ON HORSEBACK (WATER-COLOUR) IN POSSESSION OF MRS TRENCHARD COX

John Linnell, Henry Gastineau and Samuel Palmer were in his circle of acquaintance; and among the friends who helped him in the provinces were, in Liverpool, R. H. Grundy, a printseller and amateur water-colour painter, and in Birmingham Edward Everitt, his pupil and an amateur painter; Joseph Gillott, who spent on works of art a considerable proportion of the fortune he made out of the manufacture of steel pens; Charles Birch, the collector; William Roberts, a business man and amateur painter, who would advise Cox upon the oil technique and accompany him on sketching tours; the engraver Radclyffe and his biographers, N. Neal Solly and William Hall.

*69*

In London Cox was valuably assisted by William Stone Ellis who took lessons in water-colour from 'Old Farmer Cox' and was an enthusiastic admirer of his work which he, with questionable discrimination, preferred to certain compositions by Turner. Cox's correspondence with his friends illuminates his kindly courtesy. His letters to Roberts show constant solicitation for his friend's welfare. In a letter addressed to 'My Dear Friend Roberts' from Conway, North Wales, of which the original manuscript is in the Birmingham Art Gallery, Cox advises his friend on the best way of joining him and his son at Bettws-y-Coed or Capel-Curig: 'If you put yourself into the Shrewsbury Mail at one o'clock night . . . you will be with us by three that afternoon.' The letter ends with the assurance 'I remain yr. friend, ever yours' and with a characteristically bluff postscript 'Excuse blots'. In another letter, also preserved in the Birmingham Art Gallery, Cox thanks Roberts for 'more than a brother's kindness'. 'I have no words to express the gratitude I feel for the assistance you have afforded me in acquiring some knowledge in the delightful branch of the Art, Oil Painting. . . . So far from being discouraged I like it better every day . . . tho' I know I do not paint in that regular way a proficient worker (should) . . . I cannot keep the shadow'd part of some objects quite free from opaque colour so that I am obliged to paint it to look transparent. I perceive this in many of the Old Masters, Claude for instance.' A further letter to Roberts, dealing with some business transaction at Hardwick, ends with a very typical enquiry: 'Did you send anything for the gamekeeper?' In a letter to Grundy,* written from an hotel near Lancaster in August 1838, Cox takes infinite trouble in giving his friend detailed particulars of the journey by coach which Grundy must take from Manchester in order to meet the artist at Cartmel. 'If you leave Manchester by coach called *The Water Witch* it will convey you to Preston where I believe you take the *boat*, and it will land you at *Hest Bank Hotel* (mind and *be particular in telling* the

---

* This letter is quoted in full by Mr Roe, *David Cox*, pp. 51-54.

15 PAGES FROM A SKETCH-BOOK  (PENCIL)  BIRMINGHAM ART GALLERY

boatman to put you out at *Hest Bank Bridge*) . . .' and so on, in a manner refreshingly and almost touchingly free from any egotistical preoccupations. No friends, however grand, beneficient or intellectual, could rob Cox of the simple pleasures of his family background, and one of his greatest delights was the company of his little nieces, the Misses Hills, with whom he would play 'pantomimes'.

Among the business connexions which Cox found profitable to foster was that with the publishers who continued to ask him to contribute to their books. Radclyffe proved skilfully to combine friendship with commerce: he engraved eight views in line of Dudley Castle and its vicinity between 1829–31: and reproduced plates after Cox for Roscoe's *Wanderings and Excursions in North Wales* which, on its publication by Messrs. Wrightson and Webb of New Street, Birmingham, in 1836, proved so successful that a companion volume on South Wales was planned for the following year. One of the water-colours reproduced in the earlier volume was 'Rhaidr Cwm', now in the British Museum (No. 1878/12/28/60), a rather smooth interpretation of a mountain gorge, contrasting feebly with the primeval grandeur which Turner would have given to such a scene of elemental mass and dizzying heights. Cox's publishers were canny as well as clever; they paid him from four to five guineas each for

71

his drawings, but allowed him no travelling expenses in respect of his journeys in which he covered over four hundred miles. Very occasionally Cox made original prints for sale: for instance in 1830 he etched a view of the County Hall, Hereford.

The scenes which Cox drew for publication were not confined to those which he had seen. He conformed to common practice by working up sketches by amateur artists who had travelled in foreign parts. For example, Cox executed some Indian scenes, based on sketches by Captain Elliot, R.N., which appeared in engraved form in various books of travel between 1833 and 1845. One drawing, representing an Indian Temple, together with its engraved version, is in the Birmingham Art Gallery (No. 1614/27).

In the summer of 1831 Cox went to Derbyshire where, from his comfortable lodgings at the Peacock Inn, Rowsley, he would make expeditions to paint the homes of the nobility, particularly Haddon Hall, Chatsworth and Hardwick. The romantic atmosphere of Haddon appealed especially to Cox who called it 'my favourite old Haddon' and made numerous studies of its great terrace and yew-tree walk and its huge panelled rooms. It was his custom when staying at the Peacock to walk over to Haddon whither his dinner would be sent from the inn and spread out on the table in the great hall. In the Birmingham collection are several water-colour sketches of these houses, which are interesting primarily as records. Cox was more at ease with wild nature than with the ordered works of man, and in these studies of houses he found little scope for the best elements in his art. It is evident, however, that he was impressed by the feudal way of living; and the drawings reflect a subjection to contemporary romantic fashion which suggests that the novels of Sir Walter Scott figured among the books which Mrs Cox used to read aloud to her husband when at work.*

*Two interesting sketches in the Birmingham Art Gallery (Nos. 673, 674/27) represent a piece of wall in the Long Gallery at Hardwick. They are roughly designed, like 'flats' for stage scenery, and one drawing contains a rapid sketch of a portrait, inscribed in Cox's hand: 'Lord Hartington at 15 years of age by Shee'. A series of sketches of interiors at Hardwick and Chatsworth are at Chatsworth House.

16 SEA AFTER STORM   (WATER-COLOUR)   WHITWORTH ART GALLERY, MANCHESTER

The esteem in which Cox held his own work was not based on financial value, and he never asked, nor obtained, big sums for his pictures. He had scruples about taking money from purchasers who, he thought, could ill-afford the cost and once, on insisting that a friend should take back some money, he said: 'If you are too proud to take it for yourself give it to your son as a fairing from me.' The highest price ever paid to Cox was £100 for his large oil painting 'Rhyl Sands' in the Birmingham Gallery, and during his second London period his average charge was £10 for a small drawing, and £40 for his water-colours of imperial size. Sketches and small studies he would sell for a mere trifle: possibly he would give them away. When he was painting the preparations for the opening of New London Bridge by King William IV and Queen Adelaide in August

*73*

17A LLANRWST   (CHARCOAL)   BIRMINGHAM ART GALLERY

1831, Cox set up his easel on a wharf where he was watched when at work by the owner's small son who was fascinated by the artist's procedure. Very naïvely the boy asked whether he could have the finished painting for his own. 'Oh, my lad,' replied Cox, still more artlessly, 'do you know it's worth five pounds?'

The greater breadth in treatment which marks the 'third period' of Cox's life was not achieved at once, or indeed all the time. When painting for albums or for a special kind of client he would produce highly finished water-colours, but he always aimed at an effect of richness. Most often in his more 'finished' productions Cox did not eschew the mechanical dexterity of the drawing-master: 'Chirk Aqueduct' (No. 292/25) at Birmingham, signed and dated 1833, is representative of a very large group of paintings intended purely to please; but occasionally into this kind of work Cox incorporated an

*74*

17B BOLSOVER CASTLE    (WATER-COLOUR)    BIRMINGHAM ART GALLERY

element of distinction as in the 'Landscape with Bridge', signed and dated 1801, (No. 316–1891), in the Victoria and Albert Museum, where the eye is fascinated by the delicious colour and treatment in perspective of the twisting red-brick bridge. A smaller version of this subject, undated, is in the Art Gallery at Dudley (91). Cox used a large swan's quill brush, full of colour, putting on his tints very wet, and he would hatch his paint over and over with repeated touches taking care that the preceding touches were dry; but he would not wash over the tints when once applied, as in his view this weakened the effect.

Cox's range of pigments was always limited, and he disdained to use the rarer colours considered essential by some artists. Lake, gamboge, indigo, sepia, burnt sienna, Indian red, cobalt, vermilion, light red, yellow ochre and brown pink were among his favourite colours; emerald green he seldom used (except for a touch on the draperies of figures or on the mossy coating of a stone or tree-trunk) and raw sienna or Chinese white very rarely. For a great part of his life he employed only the old 'cake' colours which he ground in saucers, but later he used the more recently invented 'moist' colours. Often on wet days, and when on holiday, he would work in the house at several drawings at the same time. Hall* tells how he has seen the artist begin by mixing a quantity of sky-colour, sufficient for three or four drawings; then he would take up one outlined sketch after another and work as fast as he could with a large brush, 'the colour running down his paper in streams, cloud forms and other peculiarities being rapidly shaped and indicated'. Whilst one drawing was drying he would proceed with another, taking each in proper order, gradually progressing with his subjects until all were finished.

Many of his outline sketches were in charcoal or black chalk, (they were often very slight, having been done when the artist was out for a walk and on the spur of the moment; occasionally even they were done indoors by lamplight). He would go over the whole sketch with plenty of colour, sometimes leaving the chalk to show through. 'Try by lamplight and don't be afraid of darks' Cox wrote to his son in 1842. 'Have your colours quite soft, and colour upon the charcoal. Get all the depth of the charcoal and be not afraid of the colour. When you look at it by daylight and clean it with bread you will find a number of light parts which have been left where the colour would not exactly adhere over the charcoal.' Cobalt was his favourite colour for the sky; and he would represent the shadowed parts of the clouds and the extreme distances of his pictures with cobalt mixed with light red, vermilion and, occasionally, a little lake and yellow ochre. From the distance he would work to the middle grounds for which he would use 'sensitive' colours such as for greenery, indigo, gamboge and lake with its varieties and for the

*A Biography of David Cox: pp.146–147.

18 THE OLD EXCHANGE AND MARKET STREET, MANCHESTER    (WATER-COLOUR)    WHITWORTH ART GALLERY, MANCHESTER

19A COUNTRY ROAD; DRIVING CATTLE   (WATER-COLOUR)   BIRMINGHAM ART GALLERY

rocks, cobalt, vermilion or yellow ochre. In the middle distance he would work over each part separately 'like mosaic'. In the fore-grounds he would place his most powerful colours, indigo, sepia and van Dyck brown. Body colour he would only use in the smallest quantity. For his personal instruction Cox would on occasion copy paintings by other artists. He reproduced Martin's 'Belshazzar's Feast', Cattermole's 'The Battle of the Bridge', and on one occasion he asked permission from Sir Robert Peel to copy 'The Avenue' by Hobbema, now in the National Gallery. At Birmingham is a small water-colour 'A Street in Verona' (No. 108/18) copied from a painting by Bonington now in the Victoria and Albert Museum.

Whilst on his journeys and expeditions David Cox would make frequent notes and quick sketches which he would keep for use in building up his exhibition pictures. Some of these finished pictures were composite landscapes expressing the essential character of a certain locality rather than being an actual representation of a particular spot. Cox's little memoranda, which he would have considered mere trivia, are among his most precious work, for they have a spontaneity which his completed work sometimes lacks. In the Birmingham collection there is a delightful series of such notes, and the subjects include trees, flowers, fish, birds, and domestic animals. Occasionally a figure subject shows Cox in an unusual mood: a slight study of a lady holding a baby at a font, p. 65, lent to the Birmingham Art Gallery by Mr M. Brown suggests that, had he so wished, Cox might have become a successful portrait painter. A series of decorations for a summer house, representing the Four Seasons (Nos. 730–3/27), now at Birmingham, are further reminders of Cox, the stage designer.

Some very characteristic studies are impressions of countryfolk. A very slight sketch done in sepia wash and colour, of two old farmers on horseback, p. 69, in the possession of the writer's wife, is a delicious vignette of rural society. One can almost hear the loud tones of conversation as the old gentlemen, both rather hard of hearing, stop to exchange the local gossip; and one feels at any moment they

19B THE MILL STREAM    (WATER-COLOUR)    WHITWORTH ART GALLERY, MANCHESTER

will jerk their reins and ride on according to their respective ways. This very eloquent trifle was probably a favourite in Cox's family as it was handed down to the artist's grand-daughter Hannah, who sold it in 1904. Two delightful studies, in water-colour, of peasant children, p. 66, inscribed and dated 'Llandudno 1853', are among a group of drawings owned by Sir Robert Witt, C.B.E., which also formerly belonged to Cox's grand-daughter. In his humorous rendering of demure childhood Cox here shows himself as a predecessor of Kate Greenaway. Also in the Witt collection are some botanical studies of thistles and dock-leaves.

Cox's sketchbooks illustrate an interesting aspect of his methods of work. Some of them contain rapid records of what he saw on his journeys: the free, immediate draughtsmanship suggests the impulse of enthusiasm with which Cox would whip out the book from his pocket and dash away a sketch with his pencil. Such an impression of controlled speed is given in the little sketch book in the Victoria and Albert Museum of which one page represents a country road, very slightly but tellingly indicated in pencil and inscribed '4 miles on the road from Kirby Stephen to Sedburgh'. Other sketch books were obviously for more formal purposes as they contain finished, rather conventional sketches, either done for the benefit of students or partly done or finished by the students themselves. On the first page of one of three such sketch books in the Birmingham Gallery is written in David Cox's hand: 'These studies are for the use of students and must be kept intact.' Some of the sketches in these books are in monochrome which was intended to be covered with transparent washes. Solly (pp. 269–270) mentions a number of sketches, taken from sketch books of various dates, which Cox left to his executor, Mr Stone Ellis. Solly refers especially to a water-colour drawing representing an old woman driving geese across Dulwich Common. This is now in the Art Gallery at Dudley, together with other water-colour sketches including some of an unusual type representing military scenes. One wonders whether these latter, which

IV  THE WELSH FUNERAL (OIL) BIRMINGHAM ART GALLERY

are undated, are in any way connected with Cox's period of residence at Farnham Military College. Two books containing a number of free, delicate sketches of scenes near London in Kent, Wales, and Scotland, belong to Mr Matthew B. Walker of Wolverhampton. These, like the sketches at Dudley, were bought from the sale of Catharine Ellis, the daughter of Cox's executor; and may be those which are referred to by Solly (p. 269) as 'gems'.

Some of David Cox's broader sketches of scenery and seascape are almost impressionist in their freedom of handling. 'A Water Mill' (No. 249), 'Sea after Storm', p. 73 (No. 982), both at the Whitworth Art Gallery, Manchester, and 'Mountainous Landscape: Evening' (No. 829/07) at Birmingham are little lyrics in paint; and the unfinished study of 'Hares Feeding' (No. 332/07), in the Birmingham Collection, is a charming indication of Cox's intimate understanding of wild life.

Another attractive type of sketch was made by Cox in pencil touched with white on blue 'grocer's' paper. The Birmingham Gallery contains a number of slight studies in this medium, one of these representing Aston Hall, Birmingham, a magnificent Jacobean mansion, formerly the home of the Holte family and now used as a museum. Some of Cox's charcoal sketches on white paper are among his strongest work, and a few show a freedom of treatment and an interpretation of atmosphere equal to Cox's most significant achievements in water-colour. A particularly vivid example is 'Llanrwst', p. 74 (No. 753/27) in the Birmingham Gallery in which the animated life of a village street is conveyed by a few telling lines and eloquent blobs of charcoal. Other charcoal sketches, in the same collection, anticipate in dramatic intensity the furious dexterity of van Gogh.

In 1834 Cox went to Derbyshire, Cheshire, Lancashire and Yorkshire, and visited Bolsover Castle which he frequently sketched. A water-colour of Bolsover, p. 75 (No. 334/07) in the Birmingham Gallery, in spite of being unfinished, has an airy grandeur recalling the work of Turner. The following year Cox returned to these counties

F

and stayed for a while with his sister near Manchester. On one of these family visits he painted the exquisite 'Old Exchange and Market Street', p. 77, now in the Whitworth Art Gallery, Manchester. This water-colour is undated but it probably is a fairly early work (between 1820 and 1830) as it has a delicacy which suggests the eighteenth century convention rather than the more florid style later adopted by Cox. The façades of the houses have the effect of crumbling stone such as Girtin (in his Paris sketches) and Prout could convey.

In 1836 Cox discovered the Scotch wrapping paper (intended for wrapping up reams of better quality paper) on which he was to execute much of his later work.* He obtained the first few sheets by chance at Grosvenor and Chater's, and was advised that the Excise mark 84B indicated that it was manufactured at Dundee. Impulsively, he ordered a ream which to his amazement weighed one hundred and eighty pounds, and cost eleven pounds. Cox was helped in payment by Roberts, and his initial dismay was turned to regret that he did not order more, as the paper exactly suited his needs, and he never again was able to obtain any more of equal quality.

The paper was made from linen sailcloth well bleached, and its ready absorption of colour, when used for water-colours, gave strength to his work, suited to his rapid, nervous strokes with a full, wet brush. The rough texture of the paper worried those people who looked for a smooth finish in water-colour painting: furthermore, it contained little black and brown specks. On one occasion when asked what he did with those specks if they occurred on a part of the paper on which he wanted to paint sky, Cox replied, with characteristic dash: 'Oh, I just put wings to them and they fly away as birds.' The best known example in the Birmingham Gallery showing Cox's use of the rough paper is 'Sun, Wind and Rain', f.p. 64 (No. 269/25) painted in 1845 after his return to Birmingham. Cox also did a composition in oils of this subject in 1845, the year after Turner's 'Rain, Steam and Speed'

---

* 'David Cox' paper is now a patented trade-name for a type of rough drawing paper.

20 PEACE AND WAR    (WATER-COLOUR)    BIRMINGHAM ART GALLERY

had been exhibited at the Royal Academy, which may well have set
Cox thinking afresh about the possibilities of atmospheric painting.
The water-colour of 'Sun, Wind and Rain' has all the qualities
expected of the more spectacular type of Cox's drawing: it is a powerful rendering of the driving force of nature: the wind can almost be
heard as it whistles in the trees, and the birds to cry as they wheel in
the gusty air. It has vigour, brilliancy and sparkle; yet, for the writer
at least, this painting contains an element of showmanship which is
lacking in Cox's most sensitive work, such as, for example, the
lovely, unfinished water-colour 'A Country Road: Driving Cattle',
p. 78 (No. 324/07). The better-known picture is made up from the
ingredients of a successful Cox recipe: dramatic subject and colouring
(the old woman's green umbrella is a favourite motive with Cox and
his equivalent of other artists' 'red spot'), an interpretation of nature
in a wild mood, conveyed with a sense of clever achievement. The
unfinished work is a little masterpiece of free handling and delicious,

*83*

tender harmonies of colour; it indicates an awareness of the mystery of nature which the more fussy showpiece obscures. Only occasionally do the rough-paper sketches retain the sensibility which tends to become lost in the display of virtuosity. An exception is 'The Mill Stream', p. 79, at the Whitworth Art Gallery, Manchester, which combines nobility of treatment with unobtrusive loveliness. Another very impressive study on rough paper is 'Carrying the Hay', p. 90 (No. WAG 983), also in the Whitworth Art Gallery. In this painting Cox has given his peasants working in the fields a dignity which is almost symbolic. The manner which Cox developed for his 'exhibition' pieces led to a repetition of subjects as well as of type, and his frequent use of the same titles: 'Asking the Way', 'Going to the Hayfield', 'A Windy Day' or 'The Skirts of the Forest' make difficult the identification of his pictures from exhibition lists or catalogues.

In the summer of 1836 Cox went again to Rowsley and later to Buxton to take the cure for rheumatism. Also he spent some time at Birmingham where he painted the very charming water-colour of St Philip's church, now the Cathedral (No. 557/04) in the Municipal Collection. The circumstances in which this little work was done are typical of Cox's impulsive approach to his subject. He met Charles Birch at the rooms of the Birmingham Society of Artists, then in Temple Row. They were to go to Dudley to sketch, but on leaving the building Cox was so struck by the beautiful colour of the porch of the church that he asked Birch to forgive a change of plans, and stopped to paint this picture.

In this year Cox included, among the thirty-four drawings in the Water-colour Society Exhibition, three views of Scotland taken from sketches done by his son who had been there in 1834 (Cox, himself, did not visit Scotland until twenty-one years later). He would save every spare penny for his travels, which he usually made in the summer, a fact reflected in his work which seldom represents a wintry scene. In the winter months, when he was not teaching, he would

21 GREENFIELD HOUSE, HARBORNE   (WATER-COLOUR)   BY DAVID COX, JUNIOR
BIRMINGHAM ART GALLERY

work up for exhibition the sketches he had made from nature, often painting late into the night. His few relaxations were simple; his family circle and friends, and a little light music were the enjoyments he preferred.

In 1837 Cox added Powis Castle to his list of country-seats, and paid further visits to Hardwick (where he was frightened by the bloodhounds) and Bolton. In the spring of 1838 he struck new ground at and near Hythe where he conceived the idea of painting 'Peace and War' of which there are several versions, one in water-colour being No. 272/25 at Birmingham, p. 83, in which a shepherd and his boy watch a line of soldiers in scarlet coats and bearskins as they march down a steep road below Lympne Castle. A larger and more ambitious composition of the same subject, signed and dated 1848, is at the Lady Lever Art Gallery (No. 38). Both pictures are based on sketches made on the spot by Cox in 1838 at Dungeness Bay, where the Martello towers are seen to punctuate the coastline. Cox used the same title for an oil painting (probably now in America) done in 1846 with Lancaster in the background. In August, 1838, Cox paid his usual visit to Birmingham on his way to Rowsley, and on this occasion he had hoped to be accompanied by John Sell Cotman, who failed in his engagement at the last moment. An interesting development in English water-colour painting might indeed have taken place if the great East Anglian master had gone to the Midlands in such auspicious company. The comradeship between Cox and Cotman resulted in mutual admiration of their works. Cox copied Cotman's 'Blue Afternoon' which is now in the National Museum of Wales, and 'The High Street at Alençon' (No. 28/08) at Birmingham was once in Cox's possession. Some of Cox's paintings have indeed characteristics in common with Cotman, particularly a lovely water-colour at Birmingham 'On the Wye' (No. 333/07) in which Cox has made a somewhat similar use of flattened masses and eliptical forms.

1840 was a climacteric in Cox's career, for he then took up the serious study of oil painting. He was introduced by George Fripp to the painter W. J. Müller, who had recently returned from the Middle East, and impressed Cox with his manipulation of the oil medium. It was characteristic of Cox that he had no misgivings in placing himself, a man in the late fifties, under the tutelage of a painter nearly thirty years his junior; but his experiences with Müller rewarded his humility. Müller was astonishingly deft with his brush; he was usually left-handed but in moments of extreme excitement he would work with both hands at once. Cox was much struck by Müller's speed and efficiency and, without a tinge of professional jealousy, would urge his friends to purchase Müller's work.

This desire to become an oil painter induced Cox to take another drastic decision. For some time he had considered leaving London where he was oppressed by teaching and harried by dealers. In June 1840 he took a holiday away from his usual haunts. He visited Blackpool which he appears to have found uncongenial, but which inspired him to paint the gay and attractive little water-colour 'Blackpool Sands' (No. 274/25) in the Birmingham Gallery. On his way he passed through Liverpool where he may have painted the fine 'Old Pier-head, Liverpool' (No. 3302) now in the Lady Lever Art Gallery.

22A METCHLEY, HARBORNE    (CHARCOAL)    WHITWORTH ART GALLERY, MANCHESTER

On his return to London Cox made plans for retirement. At last the burden of professional duties could be cast off. His son, who was married and successfully established in London, could take over his pupils and David could retire with his wife to spend his old age in the surroundings of his youth. A house was found at Harborne, near Birmingham, not far from his friends Birch and Roberts; and it was made ready for occupation in the midsummer of 1841.

As usual in this latest critical time Cox's kindness to his friends was repaid by their assistance. Roberts allowed Mrs Cox to obtain at his warehouse such hardware goods and domestic commodities as fenders, fire-irons and kitchen utensils as were awkward to bring down from London. A Mrs Wilmot sent Mrs Cox a hamper of biscuits 'enough to feed half-a-dozen children for six weeks' and David junior, with his wife Hannah, eased the circumstances of departure by moving into the parents' home at Kennington.

The Coxes' few possessions were taken to Birmingham by road, by Messrs Pickford; and they, themselves, with the faithful Ann, went by train. Perhaps as he travelled homeward, at what may have seemed an incredible speed, Cox had wistful memories of that eventful journey to London some thirty-seven years ago when he and his mother bumped along the high road in a mail coach. The apprehension he felt then must now have been replaced by a looking forward to a period of peaceful fulfilment when he could study nature as an artist and not with a view to earning a living. Already Cox was making delightful plans for his new life: a series of grand new oils; exhibitions in London; carefree trips to Wales; pleasant visits to and from his friends; and children's parties in the gardens at Harborne with pink and white sugary cakes, made by Mrs Cox (who was noted for her skill in baking), and plenty of raspberries and cream.

*Study of cattle*

# V

# BIRMINGHAM
## *1841-1859*

IT SEEMS A STRANGE PARADOX THAT DAVID COX, TIRED OF the bustle of London, should have sought the healing company of Nature in Birmingham, but the choice of Harborne provided a satisfactory compromise. In the mid-nineteenth century this dormitory area was still a village, some two and a half miles from town. Greenfield House, the Coxes' home, was pleasantly situated in a lane near Harborne church and vicarage, which even now retain their atmosphere of rural England. The house still stands but in a much altered state, the red brick having been stuccoed and the residence divided in two sections. From his windows Cox must have enjoyed the views of kindly open country stretching out in the direction of Hagley. A charcoal drawing 'Metchley, Harborne', p. 87, in the Whitworth Art Gallery, Manchester (No. M.W.I.1321) shows harvesters at work in the fields near Cox's house. Greenfield House, p. 85, as may be supposed from numerous drawings of it by David Cox and his son, was roomy and comfortable, but the furnishing was sparse and austere, all the chairs being upright with cane seats. In the painting-room there was little except the bare necessities and Cox's easel and sketching table,* which, during the winter for the sake of warmth, he would transfer to the parlour where he had built a bow window

*The easel, table and a mahl-stick given to Cox by Müller are now in the Birmingham Art Gallery. A chair which belonged to the artist is the property of the Royal Society of Birmingham Artists.

22B CARRYING THE HAY    (WATER-COLOUR)    WHITWORTH ART GALLERY, MANCHESTER

looking on to the garden. Here he could look at the view as he painted; also he would see on the walls of this room his few oil paintings by other artists, including two by Müller. While avoiding luxury the Coxes lived in circumstances of unpretentious plenty; and an indication of the amplitude of their times is given in a letter to his son where he praises the commodities of the old-fashioned kitchen containing 'plenty of hooks to hang up bacon and hams'. On the garden* which in the artist's day extended from Greenfield Lane (now Road) to the present High Street, Cox lavished a care which was the outcome of his creative instinct. He planted an avenue of filberts and nut-trees and grew a willow from a cutting taken from the tree overhanging Napoleon's grave at St Helena (the willow was blown down some twenty years ago). Cox showed a special predilection for broad-leaved plants such as rhubarb and Scotch thistles: a taste which is seen in many of his later pictures, as for instance 'Sun, Wind and Rain' in which the foreground is a low bank massed with

* Some of the original garden buildings may be seen from Bull Street, Harborne.

dock-leaves. As well as his favourite hollyhocks Cox cultivated other old-fashioned herbaceous flowers and was especially proud of his tulips which he would exchange with his friends.

Such then was the setting in which the Coxes, with their servant and their cat, prepared to meet the autumn of their lives. Their desire for retirement was such that they kept the street door always locked, and used the garden entrance for their few warmly welcomed visitors. The daily routine was constant. Soon after breakfast Cox would begin painting until about midday when he would walk in the garden, visit a neighbour, or occasionally go on a shopping expedition to Birmingham with a boy to carry the basket. After dinner, at half-past one, he would work again until tea-time when friends would drop in and look at his canvases and portfolios. He particularly befriended artists and on occasion would look out earlier works of his own to aid their efforts to paint a scene which he had, himself, attempted. In the evening, when the lamp was lit, Cox would like to make in charcoal or water-colour, rough sketches which he would call 'cartoons', whilst Mrs Cox, now getting rather old and infirm, would sit in her favourite high-backed chair and read aloud from the newspapers and magazines; thus affairs of topical interest would penetrate the quiet house through the pages of the *Examiner* and the *Illustrated London News*. On Sundays Cox would not paint and the day would be spent quietly, with a visit to Harborne Church in the morning and a reading from the Bible before bed.

This absence of 'temperament' distinguishes David Cox from the popular conception of an artist and makes him comparable with Anthony Trollope, who also worked according to a set routine, to which he was so wedded that he wrote portions of his novels in the train whilst making journeys in connexion with his work as a civil servant.

As soon as he was settled at Greenfield House, Cox steeped himself in the study of oil painting, and the seriousness with which he took up this medium, comparatively late in life, is revealed in his

*91*

correspondence. In a letter to his son, written from Harborne in December 1845, he gives elaborate details of his method. The dark passages are put in, he advises, with transparent colours which, if mixed with some fine powder of plaster of Paris, acquire a substance without being made to look opaque. 'For greens or half-lights' he enjoins 'also use a little plaster of Paris, and so on till you come to the high lights when you may use Naples yellow, lemon yellow and yellow ochre.'

White must be cautiously used 'only in such sparkling touches as Constable did; but there are occasions when white *must* be used, in very pale greens on dock-leaves, etc., etc.'. As in his instructions upon water-colour, Cox opines that in oils certain distances need certain colours: light red and cobalt for extreme distances; bitumen and Prussian blue for the foreground. He emphasizes the use of *terra verde* ('a most useful colour') but warns against the use of Indian red, especially in the greens. Sometimes he used his palette knife to flatten those parts of his foliage which appeared too fussy or, as he would put it, 'touchy'; and his wonderful suggestion of a breeze blowing across the landscape was given by what he called a 'sidelong touch' in the handling of leaves and herbage.

Cox's biographers, Solly and Hall, writing in 1875 and 1881 respectively, refer to the excellent state of preservation of his oil paintings which they still notably retain. Hall tells that Cox seldom used a mahl-stick but preferred to keep his hand and arm free, resting one hand on the other when special steadiness was required in the finishing of figures and small details. As in water-colours he liked a full brush and, when painting from nature, he would work on small milled boards, two of which he would usually keep in a tin box on slides so that when wet they were prevented from touching. His normal price for a small oil sketch was £7. 10s. and if the circumstances were exceptional he would raise the price to £8.

Modest as ever, Cox could not believe that his oil painting would satisfy the exacting standards of the 'oil men', whom he felt must have secrets they refused to impart to him. He felt uneasy when any oil painters examined his pictures carefully ('My pictures are not intended to be smelt' he growled, with nervous irritation on one occasion); and if he sent an oil painting to an exhibition he was on edge until he saw how it looked when hung. Cox's fear was that his oils looked 'chalky'. Many paintings indeed he kept hidden away in a cupboard under the studio staircase. His misgivings were shared by some of his fellow-artists, including William Hunt who wrote: 'The water-colour men are taking to oil. . . . I am fearful Cox will never get the same qualities in oil that he gets in water, and which quality was a great charm in his works.'

Cox felt a sympathy with the oil medium which made him regret that he had not used it sooner. In a letter to David of the 2nd April, 1843, he confesses these regrets. 'There is not half the trouble with oil as with water-colours. I should never again touch water-colours only for my honour and duty to the Society I belong to. . . . In oil you may make alterations but in water-colours you are subject to spots in the paper, and if you alter, the paper becomes so rough that you lose all atmosphere. . . . Give me oil. . . . I only wish I had begun earlier in life.'

Cox soon grew tired when painting large pictures, and the majority of his work in oils are consequently small in size. He seemed to be reluctant to finish a picture which had been bespoken and to lose interest as soon as a prospective purchaser had written his name on the back of a canvas. 'I am at best a very slow oil painter and that will be some excuse' was his apology for delay in fulfilling a commission from a certain Mr Spiers. The Birmingham Art Gallery contains an interesting series of the more intimate oils. 'A Cottage Interior', p. 94 (No. 2494/85) was painted in 1840 and shows the artist still feeling his way with the medium. The powerful effects he was to obtain have not yet appeared in this quiet domestic interior, reflecting the influence of the Dutch School; nor has Cox reached his full development in the 'Welsh Shepherds' (No. 2513/85), painted about the same time and very loose in handling and reticent in tone. Also painted about 1840, on unprepared millboard, is a study of 'Fish; Skate and Cod', p. 97 (No. 666/27) at Birmingham, which shows Cox attracted to a subject which has caught the attention of many painters, from the Dutch painters of still life to the fantastic Anglo-Fleming of the present day, Baron James Ensor.

On the smaller oils Cox would often prefer to work by artificial light. 'When I paint in oil or water-colour by lamplight, ' he wrote, 'my picture is always broader in effect, more brilliant and often better and more pure in the colour of the tints.'

Cox's preoccupation with the oil medium did not prevent him from making his sketching expeditions. Very soon after his arrival at Harborne he went to Bolton Abbey, which, up to 1846, he had

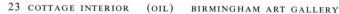
23 COTTAGE INTERIOR   (OIL)   BIRMINGHAM ART GALLERY

94

visited probably more frequently than any other place, and after he ceased to go there he used it as a subject for his painting both in oils and water-colour. A water-colour of Bolton Abbey exhibited in 1847 was regarded by some of Cox's fellow-members of the Society as 'the very best drawing he had made'. As well as making these journeys into the country Cox continued to go to London for the exhibitions. In Birmingham he broke his resolution not to teach by giving lessons to a solicitor from Worcester, Mr Taunton, who was so enthusiastic that Cox's heart softened and he took him as a pupil for some years.

The country which most appealed to Cox was North Wales, although until 1846 he continued intermittently to visit Derbyshire and Yorkshire. When in July 1842 (the year in which he was elected a member of the Birmingham Society of Artists) he went for a fortnight to Bolton, he took with him a portable easel and materials for painting in oils in which, having the subject before him, he felt he made rapid progress. Whether because in his advancing years he became disinclined to make long journeys or whether because Wales suited his requirements as an oil painter, Cox became more and more wedded to that country and after 1844 he made his principal centre Bettws-y-Coed. The grandeur of the Welsh scenery appealed to him and, in writing to his wife from London in 1842, he describes his nostalgia for Wales with its 'truly rural state of nature and the dear PEAT': a homely and very characteristic comment from Cox who liked the smell of peat and would buy it, when living in London, from hawkers' carts and burn it on his hearth, enjoying the scented smoke.

In 1843 Cox had a severe illness, and went to recuperate with his sister at Sale, near Manchester, but his enjoyment was impaired by bad weather and his feeling poorly ('I feel feeble and all at once get very old' he wrote to his friend, Roberts). The following year he sent two pictures in oil to the Royal Academy, and went up to London to see them on view. On this occasion he was much impressed by seeing at Messrs Robson and Millers in Long Acre moist colours *in bottles* and with indiarubber stoppers, evidently an innovation. In July he stayed at the Swan* at Bettws-y-Coed which he was to visit almost every year till 1856, three years before his death. In the winter of 1844–45 Cox was ill with bronchitis from which he recovered only just in time to go to London in the spring to see the sixteen drawings he had sent to the 'Old' Water-colour Society. At this time he was much concerned with his ill-health and thought of taking some small property at Bettws, where the sweet mountain air would do him good; it may have been this malaise which caused him to feel dissatisfied with the hanging of his pictures, particularly the one of 'Haddon Hall' which was skied. Later, in the summer, Cox paid his last visit to his favourite Rowsley, going from there to Bettws-y-Coed.

This year 1845 closed with a bitter sorrow, as Mrs Cox, who had been failing for some time, died on the 23rd November and was buried in Harborne Churchyard. In his wife Cox lost the perfect helpmeet; in addition to her domestic efficiency she gave him a needed mental stimulus, and was an excellent critic of his work: in fact, occasionally Cox would complain of the severity of her standards, to which protests Mrs Cox would reply that only she cared enough about his work to be in a position to tell him when he fell short of his best. At times Mrs Cox would act as a model for her husband and he would throw a cloak or shawl round her which would give him the necessary colour-notes for a figure study. Cox accepted his wife's death with his unquestioning belief that all God's actions are ultimately for the best, and he plunged himself more deeply into his work.

After this crisis Cox's artistic personality assumed a seriousness which was not always beneficial to his work. His water-colours tended to become more obviously 'exhibition pieces', conforming either to the type of smooth and showy 'drawing-room pieces' representing a picturesque view such as the 'Junction of the Llugwy and the Con-

---

* The Royal Oak which Cox was later to make his headquarters at Bettws did not exist at the time of this visit. According to Solly Cox had stayed at the Swan as a young man and had started a sketching club there.

24 STUDY OF FISH: SKATE AND COD   (OIL)   BIRMINGHAM ART GALLERY

way' (No. 267/25) in the Birmingham Collection, or the 'rough paper' compositions with all the usual ingredients: an old person in difficulties in a blustering wind, frightened sheep, a distressed shepherd, a galloping horse, contorted tree-trunks and 'cabbagey' vegetation, as are typified in such paintings as 'The Frightened Flock' (No. 276/25) at Birmingham, 'Homeward Bound' at the Whitworth Art Gallery, Manchester, and 'The Belated Traveller' in the Victoria and Albert Museum.

To the period between 1846 and 1856 belong Cox's best-known oil paintings which, like the water-colours, are most completely successful when on a small scale. Perhaps the most widely admired is 'A Windy Day', p. 100 (No. 2666) in the National Gallery. The wind seems to blow straight across this picture, and the old woman as she

G

hobbles over the common in the teeth of the wind is not a mere artist's cliché, but a human being battling against the elements. 'Sheep Shearing' (No. 2508/85) at Birmingham, signed and dated 1849, has a satisfying compactness of design and a lovely translucency of paint (a very similar version of this picture but in water-colour is in the British Museum). Sometimes for his oil pictures Cox would use the reverse side of the canvas, as he thought by this method he could obtain a freer effect.

On a larger scale Cox's oil paintings are inclined to become dull and pompous, as is 'The Gathering of the Flock' (No. 100) in the Manchester City Art Gallery. The well-known 'The Skirts of the Forest' (No. 2484/85) at Birmingham, signed and dated 1855–56, painted for Mr David Jones for the sum of £40 and later sold with 'The Welsh Funeral' for £3,300, is one of several versions, by the artist, of Sherwood Forest: it is a good solid 'Cox' but uninspiring. One of the most ambitious in scale of Cox's oil paintings is 'Rhyl Sands', p. 107 (No. 2489/85) at Birmingham, signed and dated 1854–5, for which the artist was paid his highest price (£100) and which was later sold in 1875 for £2,300. This is a distinguished painting (the outcome of numerous sketches made at Rhyl in the summer of 1854), but its composition is too slight for its size, and the picture consequently lacks the grip of some of Cox's less pretentious works.* The story that Cox's pupil Burt took a hand in its completion may not be without foundation. Preferable far is the very lovely earlier version of 'Rhyl Sands', p. 106 (No. 1917/170), in the Manchester City Art Gallery, which is more lightly painted and has almost an impressionist sparkle, anticipating that of Boudin. A beautiful incompleted work at Birmingham is 'The Missing Lamb' (No. 2517/85), p. 108, painted about 1852, which gains from its lack of finish a delicacy of touch giving the appearance of a large scale water-colour. In this painting Cox shows an unusual mastery of free draughts-

*When this picture was restored it was found that the design had been first sketched in water-colour on the canvas.

manship with the brush; it is most boldly designed with only one small figure of a girl, almost lost among and yet providing a centre to the silvery crags and boulders which tower over her as she points to a wounded lamb on the ledge of rock below. A similar composition, in water-colour, called 'The Missing Flock' is in the collection of Mr Walter Turner at Solihull.

Cox's oil paintings were very much in demand by his friends, and he often was asked for copies of the more popular subjects. On principle Cox never painted an exact replica, but usually made some slight alteration in the grouping or treatment of sky and trees. One of the best-known of his compositions in oils, 'The Skylark' (1849), now in the collection of Mr F. J. Nettlefold, was not repeated in that medium. A similar, but by no means identical, water-colour with the same title was executed and exhibited in the preceding year and is in the same collection. Both the water-colour and oil (see *Nettlefold Collection Catalogue*, pp. 134, 136) were acclaimed by Cox's friends as among his happiest compositions; both pictures represent a group of children watching the hovering flight of a lark and both are characteristically English in their sentiment and freshness. At a dinner held in Liverpool in 1875 to celebrate an exhibition of Cox's works, the artist's friend Radclyffe singled out 'The Skylark' for special praise, saying 'Who could ever cage a lark after looking on that picture?'

Only occasionally did Cox achieve a painting in oil or water-colour which stands by itself as a memorable work of art and is not a significant example of a type which he developed or improved. Such an exception is 'The Welsh Funeral', perhaps Cox's masterpiece. There are some six variants of this picture, of which the example (No. 3/43), f.p. 81, in the Birmingham Gallery, dated 1848, is probably the earliest in oil and was painted for Charles Birch. A very imposing water-colour, exhibited in 1850, is in the Whitworth Art Gallery, Manchester; and a version in oil, rougher in texture, fresher in colouring and less orderly in composition than the example at Birmingham is in the National Gallery.

100

In his handling of this subject Cox at last has transcended the realistic by the symbolic. He was inspired by an incident which occurred whilst he was staying at Bettws-y-Coed when he attended the funeral of a young girl which, in accordance with local custom, took place shortly before sundown. The symbolism is discreetly indicated in the example at Birmingham: the bell-turret is illumined by the hopeful glow of sunset; and children are playing with poppies, the blossoms of sleep. One of the mourners, represented as an old man with a mourning hat-band, is said to be Cox himself, who was personally grieved by the untimely death of this young relative of his host at the Royal Oak. These details of subject are, however, of secondary interest: the main beauty of the painting lies in the unity of its design, the warm romantic colouring and the implied movement of the procession of mourners who, grouped closely together, seem to shuffle slowly, silently and sadly, towards the chapel door. The picture possesses an elemental quality conveyed by the artist's sincerity; it has the timeless tenderness of Wordsworth's 'Lucy' poems: the cycle of life and death is taking place in accordance with God's inevitable design, and the dead girl, joined with eternal Nature, now

'. . . neither hears nor sees,
Roll'd round in earth's diurnal course
With rocks and stones and trees'.

In spite of his later work becoming more studied Cox remained the unassuming, impulsive person he had always been. There are various stories of him at this time told lovingly but with some amusement by his friends. Once, when out for a walk and hurrying home to a meal, he stopped and drew a complete picture in the dust in the road; on another occasion he saw a potential painting in an expanse of sky reflected in a window pane. One day, when in London, he called on his friends the Cattermoles at Clapham Rise, and finding

25 A WINDY DAY (OIL) NATIONAL GALLERY

them out, left a little imaginary pencil sketch of a windmill instead of a visiting card.

Cox's visits to London and the exhibitions gave him less and less pleasure. 'London is quite BABYLON: the whirling of carriages bewilders me' he wrote to Roberts in April 1847. In this year Cox painted the 'Landscape with Windmill and Man Ploughing', p. 111 (No. 821) in the Lady Lever Art Gallery, which is almost identical in subject with an oil sketch by Constable called 'Spring' in the Victoria and Albert Museum. This sketch was engraved in mezzotint by David Lucas and published in his *English Landscape Scenery*, 1855.

Cox's happiest hours of leisure were spent either on a winter's evening enjoying a glass of wine and a half cigar as he talked, or made music, with his friends at Harborne, or spending the long summer days at Bettws-y-Coed with his easel and colour box and, when work was done, joining his cronies at the Royal Oak around a convivial pint of ale.

The journey to Bettws-y-Coed was strenuous. Cox would usually leave Birmingham by the Old Grand Junction Railway and travel by way of Chester and Rhyl to Conway. Sometimes he would leave the train at Ruabon and make his way by Llangollen. In any case he would finish the journey in an open Welsh jaunting car, the means of conveyance he preferred, as he much disliked the stuffiness and jostling of a mail-coach and still more the train, particularly when it passed through the frequent tunnels on the route to Wales. But the destination was worth the fatigue. Cox found the Robertses of the Royal Oak welcoming and understanding hosts, who anticipated his needs by kindly actions, and the scenery could be enchanting. In fine weather it was a fairy country of woods, crags and tinkling waterfalls, with little cottages nestling under the rocks and sending up spirals of sweet blue peat-smoke into the misty hills; but in storm its beauty could suddenly become sinister, the woods were then wild, the cascades roaring and the flocks would huddle for shelter on the exposed and desolate uplands.

Cox, in a 'suit of sober grey' and puffing a cigar, would lose little time before going out to sketch his favourite subjects nearby, the rocks behind the Royal Oak, the mill and salmon-trap, the heron-pool, the church and the Big Meadow.

A very fine drawing of 'The Salmon Traps', in crayon and wash, is in the Tate Gallery (No. 4311), in which Cox has treated his subject with exceptionally free handling; the trees are indicated in a series of looping curves, reminiscent of Gainsborough.

Often in his excursions Cox would meet artists to whom, if inexperienced, he would not hesitate to give advice; on one occasion when he saw a young painter working timorously with a little colour and very small brushes Cox could not refrain from exclaiming: 'Don't be afraid, sir; dab, dab, DAB it, sir.' Another time he befriended a young artist in whom he saw promise by paying for his board and lodging at the Royal Oak, thereby enabling him to extend his stay in Bettws-y-Coed.

Cox's genial manner endeared him to the residents of the Royal Oak, among whom was an amateur painter, earnest and very stout, known to the visitors as 'Fat Hoyle'. Cox would assist Hoyle in his sketches which he liked to exhibit in the inn as entirely his own work. Hoyle was equally enthusiastic—and probably as prone to exaggerate —about his talent for fishing; and it is possible that Cox's sketch of a portly angler, p. 68 (No. 724/27), in the Birmingham Art Gallery is a study of this rather absurd person. The villagers of Bettws-y-Coed also learned to regard Cox with affection and respect. Boys would covet the honour of carrying his easel and sketching equipment and the old people would benefit by his charitable actions, particularly the old ladies, who would be engaged to knit him worsted stockings.

Cox added to the amenities of the Royal Oak Inn by his brush as well as by his personality. In the parlour, over a bricked-up door, he painted a fresco of 'Catharine Douglas barring the castle door with her arm' after a cartoon by Redgrave; and in 1847 he painted a sign-board in oil, representing Charles II in the oak tree at Boscobel.

Whilst at work upon the sign, he was greeted by a former pupil, Mrs Ashley, who happened to be passing in her carriage. 'Oh Mr Cox, is it really you?' she exclaimed, 'I hardly expected to see you here, mounted up so high on the ladder of fame.' Cox also drew a forest oak as a frontispiece to the visitors' book which he bought and inscribed with his name as the first entry. Cox's mode of living at Bettws-y-Coed was very simple. His favourite supper-dish was a kind of porridge known as 'crowdie' of which he liked to invite his fellow-guests to partake. On Sundays he would always go by jaunting car to the English Church at Llanrwst. Year after year his routine was much the same, although from 1852 onwards he would stay at a farm-house belonging to Mr Roberts rather than at the Royal Oak. In 1855, as well as staying at Bettws, he went for a while to Capel Curig. As Cox became feebler the excursions necessarily became less stren-uous and in 1856 he was unable to paint out of doors. This time he went to Bettws-y-Coed accompanied by his housekeeper and his picture-mounter George Priest who assiduously attended to his needs. To Priest he gave a sheet of thick Scotch paper containing a land-scape sketch on one side and a figure study on the other, with the promise that if he could separate them he (Priest) could keep one as a present. Priest succeeded by leaving the drawings in a damp cellar until the paper was so moist that he could split it with a knife. Priest kept the figure subject which he sold later for £40. Before leaving Bettws-y-Coed Cox signed the visitors book '*David Cox, September 22nd 1856*' thus recording the last occasion on which he was to visit his 'dear old Bettws'.

About 1850 Cox began what is sometimes called Cox's 'fourth period' when his work became looser and more 'blottesque'. His eyesight was failing and he felt that his hand was losing its sureness. On the 15th March, 1850, he wrote to David junior: 'My drawing upon the Scotch paper is so rough I fear I shall bring down all against me, but the paper has plagued me so I am very nervous.' Despite ill-health, he would not give in. His water-colours continued to appear at the Society which he always visited, and in 1851 he went to the Great Exhibition in Hyde Park, which he thought should be used as an opportunity to show off the English genius to foreign artists. 'I have lately been thinking,' he wrote to David in February, 1851, 'that it would be a friendly thing if our Society would give free admission tickets to all the Continental artists who will visit London this summer', and he suggested that in the method of distribution Mr Colnaghi, the dealer, and the painter, Mr Cattermole, should be consulted. In 1852 Cox visited Ludlow and painted the famous moated manor of Stokesay: he hoped to return to this historic place the following year when he was prevented by a stroke from which he never fully recovered. On a Sunday morning in June 1853 he fell in his garden at Greenfield whilst cutting some asparagus for dinner. Ann was away, but the maid Mercie rushed for a neighbour who obtained the doctor and telegraphed for Cox's son who travelled down by goods train. The initial paralysis wore off but his eyesight was permanently affected, and one of his eyelids drooped. His work, however, did not stop, but his vaguer, more impressionist manner infuriated the critics whose bitter uncomprehending statements must have pained Cox who loved his craft too well to be indifferent to the effect it made on others. 'Slobbery; spongy; inarticulate babbling' were a few of the comments made by the merciless critics whose unkindest cut of all was to suggest that the old painter was trading upon his reputation. On one occasion, when the Committee of the Water-colour Society complained that his work had become 'too rough', Cox wrote 'they forget that these are the work of the mind, which I consider very far before portraits of places': an enjoinder which shows that Cox's intention (although not always achieved) was to interpret nature rather than produce the type of academic and purely representational landscape (supplied by such an artist as Leader), with which colour-photography was later to catch up. On the whole Cox felt satisfied that his work was appreciated. In a letter written to a Mr G. Mellison in 1842, of which there is a trans-

26A RHYL SANDS   (OIL)   MANCHESTER CITY ART GALLERY

cription in the Anderton interleaved catalogue of Royal Academy exhibitions, in the Royal Academy Library, Cox wrote: 'I am fully sensible that the little merit I possess as a painter has always been fully appreciated by the public in general . . . there have been criticisms . . . some mistakes . . . but always concluding them sincere I have ever wished every person to enjoy his own opinion.'

It must indeed have been gratifying to Cox when, in 1855, his friends and admirers in Birmingham arranged to present him with his portrait. A Committee was formed and met in the rooms of the Royal Birmingham Society of Artists to discuss the ways and means, and after obtaining Cox's sanction they chose as painter Sir John Watson Gordon, the eminent Scottish Academician. The one difficulty was arranging for the two artists to meet. Sir John would not undertake a journey south, and Cox dreaded the rigours of a journey north. However, with the approval of his doctors, Cox, his son and Mr Hall, went to Edinburgh in August via Carlisle where Cox was much impressed by the Castle and attracted unwelcome attention from the sentinel who forbade him to sketch one of Her Majesty's fortresses. The fact that the soldier appeared to be venal only added to Cox's indignation. In Edinburgh Cox made various sketches, some of which are in the Dudley Art Gallery.

Cox gave five sittings to Watson Gordon who enjoyed painting him, comparing him as a sitter to Sir Walter Scott. The result, now in the Birmingham Art Gallery (No. P.L.31), p. 114, was an admirable likeness which pleased everyone except, as is frequently the case, the sitter, who felt sure that he had not such a 'long Scotch head' as Sir John Watson Gordon had given him. Perhaps the likeness was too literal to appeal to Cox whose weariness and age are emphasized,

26B RHYL SANDS    (OIL)    BIRMINGHAM ART GALLERY

even to the drooping eyelid. Whilst sitting Cox was inclined to drop asleep, when the painter would expostulate in a broad Scottish accent 'Wake up noo, Maister Corks, I am going to paint your expression'; whereupon Cox, tired and a little deaf, would turn to his son and ask 'What does he say, David?' The portrait was painted not on ordinary canvas but on Scotch sheeting which Watson Gordon's assistant prepared for him in his workshop.

27 THE MISSING LAMB    (OIL)    BIRMINGHAM ART GALLERY

The presentation took place on the 19th November, 1855, at the house of the Chairman, Mr Charles Birch of Metchley Abbey, one of Birmingham's few still surviving testimonies to the widespread vogue for 'Strawberry Hill' Gothic. A collation was served in the picture gallery which contained paintings by Constable, Turner, Etty, Maclise, and Cox's own 'Welsh Funeral'. The Chairman made an effusive speech in honour of the artist, and congratulated the subscribers on their wisdom in engaging so distinguished a painter as Watson Gordon to pay this tribute to David Cox. Then toasts were drunk, a formal address and letters of apology for absence were read,

*108*

including a letter from Mr Ruskin. Cox, overwhelmed and wearied, could say very little in response and soon begged his friend Radclyffe to take him home as it was time for him to have his milk. The portrait, bereft of the laurel wreath, which crowned it for the great occasion, was later removed to Cox's parlour in Greenfield whence it was sent, the following spring, to the Royal Academy, where Cox saw it when he went to London to give sittings to Sir William Boxall and to see some of his intimate friends such as Mr Ellis and a Mr Wilkinson. In the Water-colour Society exhibition of 1856 Cox included a version of 'The Peat Gatherers' which in oils is one of the most impressive of the series in the Birmingham Collection (No. 2504/85) and is dated 1850. To this period also belongs 'Scotch Firs' (No. P. 9–1922) in the Victoria and Albert Museum, which, although but a swift botanical note in water-colours, has the intensity and inevitability of a seriously considered work of art. An outstanding event in Cox's quiet existence was the visit to Birmingham in the summer of 1856 of Madame Rosa Bonheur, the French animal painter, who visited Cox's studio and expressed admiration for his little water-colour, on rough paper, 'The Birmingham Horse Fair', p. 115, now in the municipal collection (No. 35/09). This is, perhaps, one of Cox's most effective works: it is small in scale but spacious in effect; it shows a rich, but sensitive use of colour, and is drawn in a swift easy manner with a full brush. 'The Horse Fair' reflects no particular period, nor is it purely topo-graphical; it is a typical English scene portrayed by a quintessentially English artist.

The work of Cox in these last years of failing health has a power which reveals the determination of his spirit but a looseness of drawing betraying the weakening hand. The very late works have a dramatic intensity which was outside the scope of the artist at his prime. To this last phase belong some of his Turneresque paintings, such as those representing express trains which light up the night sky with the glow of their engines (there are two of this type at Birming-ham (Nos. 125/23 and 67/25). Most notable is the arresting water-colour in the Victoria and Albert Museum 'The Challenge', p. 120, (No. 1427–69) in which a bull, bellowing as the rain beats down on a desolate moor, vies with the roar of a thunderstorm. This painting was probably No. 179 in the Water-colour Society Exhibition of 1856 and sold the following year for £15.

Cox's last visit to London was in May, 1857, when he did the usual round of exhibitions in spite of being ill, and it must have been a relief to him to recuperate at Greenfield where he beguiled the hours by sitting in the bow-window watching a wren feeding her five fledglings in the nest she had made in a rose-bush. His great anxiety was lest his cat should disturb the birds, and until they had flown he kept 'poor puss upstairs, where she gave Mrs Fowler a good deal of trouble to carry up her food'. As he grew more infirm Cox's interest in other people did not diminish, and he never ceased to look after the poor in Harborne. Each St Thomas' Day (21st December) he would make presents of raisins, sugar and a little money and on the Queen's birthday he would send out Ann with little gifts for the old people. On one occasion he cut the best slice from a leg of mutton and sent it to an aged villager.

The last illness began with a cold taken soon after Christmas in 1858; and in January, 1859, Cox was in bed with bronchitis, suffering great discomfort, and diagnosed by his doctors as in danger. With his amazing persistence he rallied so that his son, who had come to be with him, returned to London, and in the spring not only did Cox come downstairs but he arranged for the sending of seven pictures to the Water-colour Society. The appreciation of his work by fellow artists must have given him a sense of fulfilment, for in 1858 an exhibition of his painting was held at the rooms of the Conversazione Society at Hampstead and in the spring of 1859 a more important show was planned at the German Gallery in New Bond Street.

The hopes of his recovery rose and fell. In April, 1859, he was again taken ill; in May he showed signs of improvement and was allowed up and even into the garden. Early in June Cox may have had a

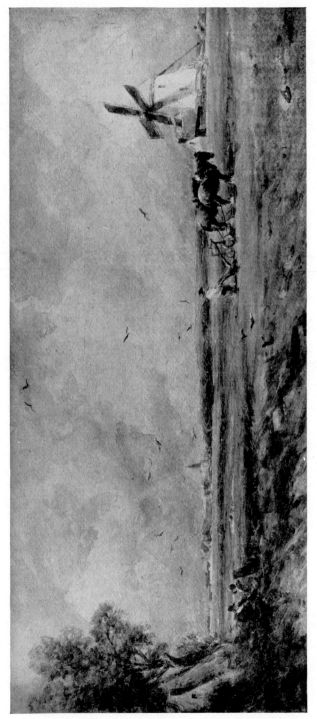

28  LANDSCAPE WITH WINDMILL AND MAN PLOUGHING    (WATER-COLOUR)    LADY LEVER ART GALLERY, PORT SUNLIGHT

*111*

presentiment that the end was very near, for one evening, when leaving his parlour on his way to bed, he exclaimed in a low, sad voice 'Good-bye, pictures! Good-bye, I shall not see you any more'; and so he took his leave of them, for he never came downstairs again. On the 6th June his son was sent for and in the morning of the next day, in the presence of David, Ann and Mercie, Cox quietly died, murmuring 'God Bless you all'. A week later, amid many friends, rich and poor, but united in their affection for him, David Cox was buried beside his wife under the chestnut trees of Harborne.

*Study of a dog*

# POSTSCRIPT

# THE PAINTER'S LEGACY

THE DEATH OF DAVID COX AT THE AGE OF SEVENTY-SIX could hardly be regarded as other than a peaceful ending to a richly prolific life, but his loss was deeply felt. His son received a large number of letters of condolence expressing appreciation of his work and character, among the correspondents being Samuel Palmer, who described the artist as a man whose intellectual and moral attainments were equally developed.

Admiration for the painter was expressed in the obituary notices which appeared in the press both local and in London.* The *Birmingham Daily Post* on June 8th, 1859, referred to Cox as one of that small band of artists who have made the English school of water-colour painters the finest in the world; and the *Art Journal* on the 1st July described him as a painter whose equal 'as an uncompromising and truthful delineator of English rural landscape we never expect to see'. *Punch*, when Cox was gravely ill, paid tribute to his services to art and nature.

As might have been expected Cox left his affairs in excellent order. He had always been careful of his money and mindful of his investments. 'With a safe 3 per cent I shall be able to paint again' he had once remarked to his bank manager. Cox made generous provision

*A copy of the memorial card, sent out to friends on the day of Cox's funeral, is preserved in the Anderton interleaved catalogue in the library of the Royal Academy.

H                                      *113*

29  PORTRAIT OF DAVID COX    (OIL)    BY SIR JOHN WATSON GORDON
BIRMINGHAM ART GALLERY

for his household and dependants. Out of his total estate of under
£12,000 he bequeathed substantial legacies to his grandchildren and
£500 to Ann Fowler.   Ever since the Hereford days Ann had invested
her savings with Mr Spozzi of the Hereford bank and in time accumu-
lated a considerable sum (in 1850, Cox, who always supervised Ann's
money affairs, sent the Spozzis an oil painting of Bolton Abbey 'for
auld lang syne'). Ann certainly combined a business sense with her
affection for her master. She used to gather up most carefully all the
sketches and rough drawings which Cox threw away as scrap paper,
and after his death she sold these for £8,000. David junior was
appointed with Mr Ellis trustee and executor of his father's estate,
and retained all his father's works, which were unsold, except those

which he left to certain intimate friends. To Ellis, Cox left a drawing of *Cader Idris*, and to Birch another drawing, selected by his trustees, both were valued at £20. To the curate of Harborne, who had been very attentive to Mrs Cox in her last illness, Cox bequeathed a water-colour of Bolton Abbey; and other kindnesses from friends were similarly commemorated.

Immediately after Cox's death a Committee was formed to consider a fitting memorial in Birmingham: Mr Hollins, a local sculptor of some repute, was commissioned to make a portrait bust to be placed in the Public Art Gallery and Mr Powell chosen to execute for Messrs Hardman a stained glass window in Harborne Church. As often occurs, the most constructive proposals did not materialize: a trust fund bearing David Cox's name for the promotion of the fine

30 THE BIRMINGHAM HORSE FAIR　(WATER-COLOUR)　BIRMINGHAM ART GALLERY

*115*

arts in Birmingham was never developed beyond the stage of discussion, and William Radclyffe was prevented from publishing a memorial volume of engravings, selected from Cox's work, by his death which occurred after only three plates were completed (these were published by the Liverpool Art Club in 1876). Had this project been realized it would in part have fulfilled Cox's intention of publishing a *Liber Studiorum* consisting of engravings done by himself from his drawings in sepia. The publication of two full-length biographies within twenty-five years of Cox's death is another measure of the esteem in which he was held by his contemporaries.

In common with many other artists Cox gained posthumous recognition. During his lifetime his works were ranked highly by his friends but drew only qualified enthusiasm from the public who, partly because of the artist's distaste for commercial publicity, did not pay highly for his pictures. For example, for two water-colours now in the Birmingham collection 'The Stepping Stones' (No. 31/08) and 'Near Bettws-y-Coed' (No. 32/08), painted in August 1846, Cox charged Mr Sherrington, who commissioned him, £8 each, and expressed the hope that he 'had not charged too high, and that they will meet with your approval.' After Cox's death, the prices began to rise, and soon even an indifferent 'Cox' acquired a 'snob' value for these collectors who felt their representation of British paintings incomplete without a picture bearing his name: a state of affairs which would have bewildered and distressed the simple-minded artist. His work was discussed, criticized and admired in widely differing social and intellectual circles. John Brett, the painter of smooth landscapes, could not appreciate Cox's atmospheric effects. 'The daubs and blots of that famous sketcher', Brett remarked, 'were just definite enough to suggest the most superficial aspect of things.' The ever-cantankerous Whistler, who disliked Cox's agitated technique, referred to him as 'old dobber'. Among those, however, who liked his paintings was Queen Victoria, under whose spell Cox, in spite of his liberalism, had fallen. A water-colour and a chalk drawing (the latter in the collection of Sir Robert Witt), representing the Queen driving in Windsor Park, bear the loyal title 'Windsor: The Queen!', p. 118. As public demand for Cox's pictures increased so did the wishful thinking of the inexperienced and the guile of the unscrupulous. Inferior works by Cox were boosted as masterpieces by proud owners, and the painstaking achievements of pupils or lesser contemporaries were sold as authentic works by the master often with a false signature attached by some dishonest middleman. Plain forgeries, too, were made, but some of these were so evident that they could only have deceived the very gullible.* The danger, indeed, of wrongful attributions is very great in the work of artists such as Cox who made their living by teaching, and there may be to-day many a proud possessor of a water-colour thought to be by Cox in which the painter's work consists only of a few skilful strokes put in to assist the owner's great-grandmother.

The interest taken in Cox's work after his death mounted so high that an exhibition exclusively of his work was held in Manchester in 1870; five years later a more extensive exhibition was organized by the Liverpool Art Club, and in 1890 a big loan exhibition took place in the Birmingham Art Gallery. A bronze commemorative medal, designed by Charles Morgan of Birmingham, was issued in 1879 by the Art Union of London.

David Cox, in the value he set on craftsmanship and truth to nature, was so much a product of his age that it is difficult to estimate how much the contemporary or younger artists who painted in the same style were influenced directly by him or responded to those same influences which had shaped his art. The popularity enjoyed by Cox's published works analysing the method by which he achieved his

*Sir Whitworth Wallis, the first Keeper of the Birmingham Art Gallery, in *The Connoisseur* in 1905 gave publicity to an organized—but very amateurish—attempt to sell false 'David Cox's,' painted on artificially stained paper. The article led to the arrest and sentence to imprisonment of a father and daughter, the former executed the forgeries and the latter sold them to ignorant persons.

31 'WINDSOR, THE QUEEN!' (CHARCOAL) IN POSSESSION OF SIR ROBERT WITT, C.B.E.

own success may have increased the number of his indirect pupils, but the very lack of individual bias in these works, which made them so useful as text-books, renders it impossible to gauge the scope of their influence. Although Cox took infinite pains with his pupils, he appears to have been an uninspired teacher or unlucky in the material which came his way. Whereas John Varley, who does not enjoy the popular reputation of Cox as a painter, numbered among his pupils such outstanding artists (in addition to Cox himself) as Linnell, Mulready, Copley Fielding, William Hunt and Samuel Palmer, Cox cannot claim to have taught any painter of more than ephemeral or local reputation. David Cox junior did little more than exploit the banal prettiness which always threatened to vitiate his father's work, and Charles Thomas Burt will be remembered, if at all, as having recorded in paint his master's funeral.* It was, however, due to the influence of Cox that G. P. Boyce, the friend of D. G. Rossetti, became a landscape painter instead of an architect.

It is more as an individual perfectly expressing the accepted tradition of English water-colour painting during the nineteenth century than as a master who altered the course of that tradition that Cox is now remembered; and such painters as Edward Wimperis (1835–1900) and Thomas Collier (1840–1891), whose aims in art were parallel with those of Cox, carried on his exact tradition but carried it no further.

In so far as David Cox appears to have been a typical product of the Victorian age he was ahead of his time, as in fact the great Queen's reign covered only the last twenty-two years of his life; but in no other way did he reveal that pioneering intrepidity of spirit which distinguishes the timeless genius from the accomplished craftsman. It was not indeed until he had established a competency of both fame and fortune that Cox attempted any novel forms of technique which, if tried sooner, might have endangered the material security of his family life.

The aims of David Cox were such as could be achieved within the frame-work of convention. He pleases but does not often surprise; and if he breaks new ground it is by conscientious endeavour rather than by revolt. The artists of the last twenty years, who may be said to express themselves in a contemporary idiom, have not been greatly influenced by David Cox whose approach to nature was spontaneous rather than intellectual, whose feet were firmly on the ground and who was more interested in the formation of earth and in what grows from it than in the caprices of light and the convolutions of form.

---

*Burt painted one of the water-colour plaques (a seascape) decorating a cabinet in veneered woods presented in 1880 to Edward Everitt, Secretary of the Birmingham Society of Artists, on the occasion of his marriage. Other pupils and friends of Cox painted medallions for this piece, including Cox's biographer, Hall. The cabinet, which is in the extreme bad taste of the late Victorian period, is at Aston Hall (but not normally on exhibition).

32  THE CHALLENGE   (WATER-COLOUR)   VICTORIA AND ALBERT MUSEUM

120

The opinions of critics on Cox soon after his death varied from official understatement to sentimental encomium, but the mean seems to have been struck by Ruskin, who, in *Modern Painters*, gave Cox the place which he deserved and has held. He praises Cox for his intimate understanding of nature, conveyed by a 'blotted' technique; for his 'melting water-colour skies . . . wild, weedy banks . . . the moisture of his herbage, the rustling, crumpled freshness of his broad-leaved weeds, the play of pleasant light across his deep heathered moor or plashing sand, the melting of fragments of white mist into the dropping blue above . . . all this has not been fully recorded except by him.' Ruskin also realized Cox's limitations, for which an uncritical public was largely answerable. In Ruskin's view Cox subscribed too easily to popular demand and developed too definite a manner. 'He paints too many small pictures, and perhaps has of late permitted his peculiar execution to be more manifest than is necessary.' He blames Cox for his 'accidental' handling which may be justified when it represents what is accidental in nature, but is without meaning when applied to forms which need a structural stability. 'In Cox the forms are always partially accidental and unconsidered, often essentially bad and always incomplete: in Turner the dash of the brush is as completely under the rule of thought and feeling as its slowest line', which is Ruskin's way of saying that Cox, in spite of his great talents, cannot be considered among those masters whose inspiration and skill combine in making works of art of the most precious order.

The figure of Cox passes across the stage of English art history not in meteoric glory nor in the flash of inventive genius, but as soberly and inevitably as one of his old farmers who, on a white horse and with a shaggy terrier to heel, will be seen jogging homeward over Cox's windy landscapes as long as English water-colours are displayed and loved.

1783    Born at Deritend, Birmingham.

1798c.  Apprenticed to the miniature painter, Fieldler.

1800    With Macready's Company at the Birmingham Theatre.

1804    Removed to London.

1805    First exhibited at the Royal Academy; went to North Wales.

1808    Married Miss Mary Ragg; removed to Dulwich Common.

1809    David Cox, junior, was born; exhibited with Associated Artists in water-colour.

1810    Became President of Associated Artists.

1812    Elected to the Society of Painters in Water-colour; went to Hastings.

1813-14 First exhibited with Society; published his *Treatise on Landscape Painting and Effect.*

1814    Became drawing master at Military College, Farnham; removed to Hereford.

1817    Went to Bath.

1819-21 Published *The Young Artist's Companion.*

1826    Paid first visit to the continent: Belgium and Holland.

1827    Removed again to London.

1829    Went to France (Calais, Amiens, Beauvais, Paris).

1830    Went to Yorkshire (Bolton Abbey).

1831    Went to Derbyshire (Rowsley, Haddon, Hardwick).

1832    Paid last visit to the Continent (Dieppe and Boulogne).

1834    Went to Derbyshire (Bolsover).

1836    First used 'Scotch' wrapping paper; went to Buxton to take the cure.

1837    Went to Powis Castle.

1838    Went to Hythe, Kent.

1840    Took lessons in oil painting from W. J. Müller; went to Blackpool.

1841    Removed to Harborne.

1842    Elected to Birmingham Society of Artists; began sketching from nature in oils as well as water-colours; went to Bolton.

1843    Had his first serious illness.

1844    First stayed at Bettws-y-Coed.

1845    Mrs Cox died.

1847    Painted sign for 'The Royal Oak' at Bettws-y-Coed.

1848    Painted 'The Welsh Funeral'.

1852    Went to Ludlow and Stokesay.

| 1853 | Had a slight stroke. |
| 1854-5 | Painted 'Rhyl Sands' for which he obtained his highest price. |
| 1855 | Went to Edinburgh in August to have his portrait painted by Sir G. Watson Gordon which was formally presented to him at Harborne in November. |
| 1856 | Went for last time to Bettws-y-Coed; was visited at Harborne by Madame Rosa Bonheur. |
| 1857 | Paid last visit to London. |
| 1858 | Began his last illness. |
| 1859 | Died at Harborne. |

NOTE: The above table refers only to some of the more significant of Cox's travels. It does not include those journeys which formed part of the normal pattern of his existence, such as his visits to his parents at Birmingham and to his sister near Manchester; nor all his journeys to the West Country and North Wales which took place at fairly frequent intervals between 1815 and 1852; nor the numerous visits to London and Bettws-y-Coed made during the last phase of his life at Harborne.

# APPENDIX B

## NOTE ON THE DISTRIBUTION OF COX'S PICTURES

The most comprehensive collection of David Cox's work in his various media is in the City Museum and Art Gallery, Birmingham, where a special attempt has been made to represent worthily the art of Birmingham's distinguished citizen. His water-colours may also be studied in the print rooms of the British Museum and the Victoria and Albert Museum and in the Whitworth Art Gallery, Manchester. The National Gallery have comparatively few oil paintings by Cox. The principal provincial art galleries contain examples of his work in oil, water-colour or pencil.

# BIBLIOGRAPHY

Books exclusively about David Cox are few. The two biographies written shortly after his death are as follows:—

N. Neal Solly: *Memoir of the Life of David Cox*, Chapman & Hall, 1873.
William Hall: *A Biography of David Cox*, Cassell, 1881.

The most recent monograph is in a limited edition, *Cox the Master*, by F. Gordon Roe (F. Lewis, 1946, price 5 guineas), which contains as an appendix a list of works by David Cox exhibited in London during his lifetime. A helpful, earlier work by F. Gordon Roe, *David Cox* ('British Artists', edited by S. C. Kaines Smith), Philip Allan, 1924, contains a useful list of paintings by Cox which may be seen in galleries open to the public.

Essays and articles about David Cox which may assist the student are as follows:—

H. M. Cundall: *David Cox as a Drawing Master*, Art Journal, 1909.
A. J. Finberg: *The Drawings of David Cox*, London (n.d.).
B. Long: *David Cox* (with list of exhibited works), Old Water-colour Society's Club, Vol. X.
A. P. Oppé: *The Water-colours of Turner, Cox and de Wint*, London, 1925.
G. R. Redgrave: *David Cox and Peter de Wint*, Sampson Low, 1891.
Whitworth Wallis: *David Cox Forgeries*, Connoisseur, May and July, 1905.

Cox's own *Treatise on Landscape Painting and Effect in Water-colours* was reprinted by *The Studio* in 1922 with an introduction by A. L. Baldry. Copies of other published works by Cox are rare.

The following general works may usefully be consulted:—

Laurence Binyon: *English Watercolours*, Black 1933 (reissued 1944).
C. R. Grundy: *Pictures and Drawings in the Collection of F. J. Nettlefold*, 3 volumes, London, 1933.
A. J. Finberg: *English Water-colour Painters*, Duckworth.
M. H. Grant: *The Old English Landscape Painters*, 2 volumes, London, no date.
C. E. Hughes: *Early English Water-colours*, Methuen, 1913.
H. J. Paris: *English Water-colour Painters* ('Britain in Pictures' series), Collins, 1945.
J. L. Roget: *A History of the 'Old Water-colour Society'*, 2 volumes, Longman Green, 1891.
W. T. Whitley: *Art in England*, 2 volumes, Cambridge, 1928.

# INDEX

*126*

DATE DUE